The Believer's Secret of Christian Love

The Believer's Secret of Christian Love

Compiled from the writings of

ANDREW MURRAY
JONATHAN EDWARDS

by Louis Gifford Parkhurst, Jr.

BETHANY HOUSE PUBLISHERS
MINNEAPOLIS, MINNESOTA 55438
A Division of Bethany Fellowship, Inc.

Published by Bethany House Publishers
A Ministry of Bethany Fellowship, Inc.
6820 Auto Club Road, Minneapolis, Minnesota 55438

Printed in the United States of America

Library of Congress Cataloging-in-Publication Data

Murray, Andrew, 1828–1917.
The believer's secret of Christian love / Andrew Murray & Jonathan Edwards ; compiled and edited by Louis Gifford Parkhurst, Jr.
p. cm. — (The Andrew Murray Christian maturity library)
Includes bibliographical references.
1. Love—Religious aspects—Christianity. I. Edwards, Jonathan, 1703–1758. II. Parkhurst, Louis Gifford, 1946– . III. Title. IV. Series: Murray, Andrew, 1828–1917. Andrew Murray Christian maturity library.
BV4639.M82 1990
241'.4—dc20 —dc20 89–48938
ISBN 1-55661-129-3 CIP

ANDREW MURRAY was born in South Africa in 1828. After receiving his education in Scotland and Holland, he returned to that land and spent many years there as both pastor and missionary. He was a staunch advocate of biblical Christianity. He is best known for his many devotional books.

JONATHAN EDWARDS was America's greatest theologian in the eighteenth century, succeeded only by Charles G. Finney in the nineteenth century. Twice he experienced revivals during his twenty-three-year ministry in Northampton, Massachusetts, and is most known for his efforts in "The Great Awakening." He became President of Princeton University and died at the age of fifty-four on March 22, 1758. His works are still studied by many today.

L. G. PARKHURST, JR., is pastor of Christ Community Church of Oklahoma City, Oklahoma, and is the editor and compiler of the Charles Finney "Principles Series" and other devotional books for Bethany House Publishers.

Books by Andrew Murray

ANDREW MURRAY CHRISTIAN MATURITY LIBRARY

The Believer's Absolute Surrender
The Believer's Call to Commitment
The Believer's Full Blessing of Pentecost
The Believer's New Covenant
The Believer's New Life
The Believer's Prophet, Priest and King
The Believer's Secret of a Perfect Heart
The Believer's Secret of Christian Love
The Believer's Secret of Holiness
The Believer's Secret of Living Like Christ
The Believer's Secret of Obedience
The Believer's Secret of Spiritual Power
The Believer's Secret of the Master's Indwelling
The Spirit of Christ

ANDREW MURRAY PRAYER LIBRARY

The Believer's Prayer Life
The Believer's School of Prayer
The Ministry of Intercessory Prayer
The Secret of Believing Prayer

ANDREW MURRAY DEVOTIONAL LIBRARY

The Believer's Daily Renewal
The Believer's Secret of Intercession
The Believer's Secret of the Abiding Presence
The Believer's Secret of Waiting on God
Day by Day with Andrew Murray

How to Raise Your Children for Christ
Revival

Preface

In *The Believer's Secret of Christian Love,* I have combined Andrew Murray's book, *The Secret of Brotherly Love,* with excerpts from Jonathan Edwards' book, *Charity and Its Fruits.* Murray's devotional style of writing will be evident throughout, but you may be pleasantly surprised to find devotional beauty and depth also in the writing of Edwards, who for many years has been known primarily as one of America's most important theologians.

The title and selection beginning each chapter are Murray's, and you will notice almost immediately his concern for the social and political implications of Christian or brotherly love. How marvelous that this missionary to South Africa would have such insight into problems that we hear so much about in South Africa and other parts of the world today! His writing is truly relevant no matter where we live.

Edward's writing comes beneath the heading, "The Practice of Christian Love." In it, he penetrates the human heart with a challenge to holiness and love, to principles and appropriate actions. Both Murray and Edwards show how the Spirit must bear the fruits of love in our lives, and how the true Christian will bear these fruits. Edwards probably wrote his work while undergoing devastating hatred and persecution in Northampton. He was eventually forced to leave the church he had pastored for twenty-three years. I believe the attitude of love he maintained during that time, as evidenced in this book, enabled him to later complete his most significant Christian literary works for posterity. His life bore testimony to the words in this book, and I hope many will be motivated to read *Charity and Its Fruits* in its entirety. The Banner of Truth edition of this work is a reprint of the 1852 edition that contains 368 pages.

Over the years, I have been blessed to read and sometimes edit and publish the works of great Christians. I am continually challenged to make every effort to live up to the works I edit with my name appended to them. The prayers I have added reflect my desire to take the teachings in each chapter to heart. All of us need to live up to bearing the name of Christ, who inspired all the authors I have edited. Every Christian book points us to Christ and to His example. The Apostle Paul said that three things abide: faith, hope and love, but the greatest of these is love. May increased faith, hope and love be the result of reading Christian classics.*

With love in the Risen Lamb,
L. G. Parkhurst, Jr.

---

*For an even more in-depth study and complete definition of love, read Charles G. Finney's *Principles of Love,* also published by Bethany House Publishers.

Contents

This is his commandment, That we should believe on the name of his Son Jesus Christ, and love one another, as he gave us commandment.

1 John 3:23

1

Love and Faith

At a certain conference, the closing service was to be held on a Sunday night. Those making plans decided to take for their subject the five great lessons to be learned from the parable of the Vine and the Branches in the Gospel of John, chapter 15. The subject of brotherly love fell to the lot of a particular minister, who tried to decline, saying, "I cannot speak on that subject. And I have never yet preached on it." He further explained, "You know that I studied in Holland. When I was there the subject of love was left to the liberals. They did not believe in God's stern justice, nor in the redemption of Christ. They preached that God is love and that is enough. Those who were orthodox Christians were not allowed to suggest that the liberals should be put out of the Church. No, everything should be permitted in love! And so, after a while, the orthodox Christians became strong in their preaching of faith in Christ. However, they mistakenly left the preaching of love to the liberals."

The Church must learn to do more than simply preach the love of God in redemption. The Church must go further and teach Christians to demonstrate the love of Christ in their hearts by showing love for their brothers. Our Lord and

Savior called this a "new" commandment. Love for our brothers in Christ must be the badge by which the world will recognize His disciples.

A great need exists for the preaching of true Christian love! Sometimes God allows bitterness to arise among Christians to show them the terrible power of sin in their hearts. Perhaps their feelings of bitterness will motivate them to shrink back from it. How greatly a minister and his people should feel the importance of Christ's command: "Love one another." If we really love each other as Christ loves us, a true life of holiness will result.

May the readings in this book help you to understand these two manifestations of love. First, the wonderful love of God in Christ to us. Second, the wonderful love in us to God and to our brothers through the Holy Spirit.

The Practice of Christian Love

Consider the nature of love: love inclines people to serve their neighbors. People who have a sincere love for their neighbors will be disposed to act with justice toward them. Real love and friendship always motivate us to serve others and never do them wrong. The Apostle Paul wrote, "Love worketh no ill to his neighbor" (Rom. 13:10).

Christian love inclines us to be truthful to our neighbors and tends to prevent lying, fraud and deceit. People are not disposed to be treacherous toward those they love. There ought to be oneness among Christians. Love will motivate us to walk humbly among others, and incline us to kind thoughts, thinking of others as better than ourselves. Christian love disposes people to honor one another. We naturally think highly of those we love.

Love will make us content in the sphere in which God has placed us. We will not covet anything that belongs to our neighbor. We will not envy him for any good thing he has. Love inspires us to be meek and gentle toward others, never treating them with hatred or violence. Love checks and restrains a bitter spirit, for love has no bitterness in it, only a gentle and sweet disposition.

Love has a sensitivity that prevents quarrels. True Christian love disposes people to be peaceable, forgiving injurious treatment, as Scripture commends: "Hatred stirreth up strifes, but love covereth all sins" (Prov. 10:12).

Prayer

Dear Heavenly Father, teach me how to love as I read your Word and see how you love. Teach me how to love as I study the life of Jesus and see how He loves. Fill me with love for you and my neighbors as your Holy Spirit fills me in my innermost being and guides me into truth for Jesus' sake. Amen.

And the grace of our Lord was exceeding abundant with faith and love.

1 Tim. 1:14

Your work of faith and labor of love.

1 Thess. 1:3.

The breastplate of faith and love.

1 Thess. 5:8.

Your faith groweth exceedingly, and the love of every one of you all toward each other aboundeth.

2 Thess. 1:3

2
Faith and Love

These verses show us the connection between faith and love in the Christian's life. Faith always comes first. Faith roots itself deeply in the love of God. Faith bears fruit in love to our brothers and sisters in Christ. In nature, the root and the fruit are inseparable. Likewise, in the realm of grace, faith and love must grow together.

Too often faith and love are separated. On the Day of Pentecost these attributes were united in the preaching and practice of the disciples. On the Day of Pentecost they demonstrated a powerful faith toward the Lord Jesus Christ with a fervent love for one another. Peter's sermon could be summed up thus: "Believe in the name of Jesus Christ and you shall receive the gift of the Holy Spirit." Naturally, the result followed: "And all that believed were together, and had all things in common. . . . And the multitude of them that believed were of one heart and of one soul" (see Acts 2:44; 4:32).

During the Reformation a powerful movement took place to establish the doctrine of justification by faith. Yet, at the same time, among the preachers and the leaders of the Reformation there existed an amazing lack of love! So the world was not taught the lesson that God's love was all-powerful to sanctify the whole life of a person.

Let this thought sink deeply into your heart: "The grace of our Lord was exceeding abundant with faith and love." As we cultivate *faith in God's love,* our hearts will be *filled with love to the brethren.* The genuineness of our faith in the love of God will be shown by love in our daily lives.

May God help us from day to day by faith to bear the fruit of this love. May we at all times be living examples of its truth and power, thereby blessing others.

The Practice of Christian Love

Love will dispose people to act mercifully toward their neighbors when they are under any affliction or calamity. We are naturally inclined to sympathize with those we love when they are afflicted. Love motivates people to give to the poor, to bear one another's burdens, to weep with those who weep, as well as rejoice with those who rejoice.

Love inclines us to fulfill our obligations to one another. Love disposes us to submit to the authorities over us and give them all the honor and subjection that is due them. Love will motivate rulers to rule over their people justly. In love, leaders will seriously and faithfully seek to do good to their followers. Love will motivate people to relate in a proper way to their ministers. They will listen to their counsels and instructions. They will submit to them in the house of God. In love, they will support and sympathize with their pastors and pray for them as those who watch over their souls. Likewise, love will incline ministers to faithfully and ceaselessly seek the good of their people. Love will motivate ministers, as those who must give an account, to watch over their flock.

Love will dispose children to honor their parents, and employees their employers. This obedience will not be with eye-service, but with singleness of heart and mind. Parents and employers will exercise gentleness and goodness toward their charges.

True love will thus motivate you to be responsible to God and to others. And if love does incline you to fulfill your Christian responsibilities, then love is the root and spring and comprehension of all virtues. When love is implanted in the heart, it is the principle which alone is sufficient to produce all good practice. Every right disposition toward God and others is summed up in the word *love.* Every good work comes from love as the fruit from a tree or as the stream from a fountain.

Prayer

Dear Heavenly Father, thank you for the boundless love that sent your Son Jesus Christ to live and die for me! Help me to meditate more and more upon His love and example and upon what that means for me as a Christian. Help me to love others with a fervency of heart that reflects your love for me as well as them, for the sake of your great family in heaven and on earth. Amen.

God is love; and he that dwelleth in love dwelleth in God, and God in him.

1 John 4:16

3
The Love of God

May God through His Holy Spirit teach you to cherish the unfathomable mystery of His love. Jesus said, "None is good save one, even God." The glory of God in heaven is that everything He wills and does is good. This includes two meanings of the word *good*: (1) all that is right and perfect; (2) all that makes for happiness.

The God who wills only good is a God of love. He does not seek His own. He does not live for himself. He pours out His love upon all living creatures. All created things share in God's love, because He desires that all may be satisfied with that which is good.

Love "seeketh not her own." Love finds happiness in giving to others. Love sacrifices wholly for others. Therefore, God offered himself to us in the person of His Son. And the Son offered himself upon the cross to bring love to us and to win our hearts. The everlasting love with which the Father loves the Son is the same love with which the Son loves us. This same love of the Father, Jesus Christ has poured into our hearts through the Holy Spirit. God desires that our whole life be permeated with this love's vital power.

The love of God to His Son, the love of the Son to us,

the love with which we love the Son, the love with which we love the brethren in obedience to His command, the love we have for all people so as to win them for Christ—all is the same eternal, incomprehensible, almighty love of God. Love is the power of the Godhead: in the Father, Son, and Holy Spirit. All who are members of the body of Christ possess the love of God, and this love streams forth from them to take the whole world within its compass.

Unsearchable, praiseworthy wonder of love! "He that dwelleth in love dwelleth in God, and God in him" (1 John 4:16). Oh, meditate on this wondrous love and adore the great God of Love!

The Practice of Christian Love

Above all, the work of redemption affords motives to love; and more than any other work of God, it reveals the wonderful depth of God's love. When the gospel speaks of God the Father and of Jesus Christ, it dwells principally upon love. The gospel brings to light the love eternally existent between the Father and the Son, and it declares how their love is revealed in many ways to us.

The gospel reveals Christ's love for His Father and the wonderful fruits of that love. He suffered and accomplished great things in obedience to His Father's will. In love, He upheld the honor of His Father's justice, law, and authority as the great moral Governor. The gospel reveals how the Father and the Son are one in love so we might know how to be one with them and with one another.

God the Father and God the Son are clothed with love. They sit on a throne of mercy and grace, encompassed about with a great light and glory, which is love.

A true Christian is distinguished by love. All that is of value in his life is summarized in love. The true light of heaven in the soul radiates warmth, which is love. Divine knowledge and divine love go hand in hand, as a view of divine things always excites love in the human soul.

True discoveries of the divine character incite us to love God more, uniting our hearts in love to Christ and inclining our souls to flow out in love to God's people and to all mankind. When we experience a right belief and true trust in the excellency and sufficiency of Christ, such belief and trust is accompanied by love, and we experience true comfort and spiritual joy.

Prayer

Dear Heavenly Father, continue to reveal more of yourself to me each day. Keep me from being a passive receiver of divine truth. Inspire me to love you more as I comprehend your character. Motivate me to share the full gospel of salvation with others. Help me to truly love those who do not know you, even though often these people are the most unlovable. Fill me with your love and concern for them, and open a door for me to reach them, for Jesus' sake. Amen.

The love of Christ constraineth us.

2 Cor. 5:14

4
The Love of Christ

Every being in heaven knows God's love. He sent His Son into the world to make known His everlasting love to us. In heaven, God exists in the glory of His love. All His angels are as tongues of fire, overflowing with praise and worship through the power of His love that fills them. Similarly, God desires that on this sinful earth, His love should take possession of people's hearts and thereby accomplish His purposes.

The Lord Jesus Christ became man and lived out the example of how God wins the world to himself through love. Jesus displayed the love of God to the poor and needy, the unbelieving and rebellious. He demonstrated God's compassion through His miracles, which relieved suffering and pain and overcame death. He subdued the hearts of sinful people with His genuine interest in their lives and love for their eternal souls.

For the same purpose, our Lord chose His disciples—to learn from Him and to be filled with His love. He gave on the cross the greatest example of love that the world has ever known: Without sin himself, He took our sins upon himself and bore the suffering and shame of a criminal and the scorn of His enemies so friend and foe alike might experience God's eternal love.

And then, after He had ascended into heaven, He gave the Holy Spirit to indwell His people and to shed abroad this love in their hearts. The disciples, impelled by the love of Christ, in turn offered their lives to make His love known to others.

Oh, Christian, think this over! God longs to have your heart wholly filled with His love. Then He will be able to use you as a channel for His love to flow out to your fellow-man. Let us say with the Apostle Paul: "The love of Christ constraineth me" (Dutch version—*urges*). Say to yourself: "I can be satisfied with nothing less. I will sacrifice everything to secure a place for this great love in the hearts of men."

The Practice of Christian Love

Love is the life and soul of practical faith. In a merely speculative faith, love is conspicuous by its absence. A truly practical or saving faith is light and heat together, or rather, light and love. A speculative faith is only light without heat; therefore, it is vain and good for nothing simply because it lacks the spiritual heat of divine love. A speculative faith consists only in the assent of the understanding; but in saving faith there is also the consent of the heart. A speculative faith is no better than the faith of devils, for they have faith only insofar as it can exist without love: believing while they tremble!

A truly spiritual consent of the heart cannot be distinguished from the love of the heart. If your heart consents to Christ as Savior, then you must have true love for Him as Savior. If your heart sincerely consents to the way of salvation through Jesus Christ, then you must love Christ, His way of salvation, and rest in Him. The act of choice or election in true saving faith is an act of love. You must embrace Jesus Christ as your dearest Friend.

Faith is a duty that God requires of everyone. We are commanded to believe; therefore, unbelief is a sin forbidden by God. Faith is a duty required in the first commandment, and it is comprehended in the great commandment: "Thou shalt love the Lord thy God with all thy heart." Consequently, it follows that love is the most essential attribute of true faith. Love is the very life and spirit of true faith: "faith worketh by love"; "as the body without the spirit is dead, so faith without works is dead also" (Gal. 5:6; James 2:26).

Love is the active working spirit in all true faith. Faith without love is nothing. A justifying faith is comprehended in the great command to love God. If you call yourself a Christian, where are your works of love? Do you love your fellowman? If your heart is full of love, you will find ways, or make ways enough, to express your love in deeds!

Prayer

Dear Heavenly Father, save me from a merely speculative faith and from a shallow intellectualism with respect to you and your Word. Save me from an argumentative spirit that I might confuse with a sincere desire for others to turn from error and come to the truth. Help me to demonstrate that I truly love you and others with an abiding love which comes only from daily reliance upon your Son, Jesus Christ, and the fullness of His Spirit. Amen.

The love of God is shed abroad in our hearts by the Holy Spirit, which is given unto us.

Rom. 5:5

5

The Love of the Spirit

Many Christians would confess that they lack a fervent, childlike love for their heavenly Father! They would also admit that they do not obey Christ's second great commandment. They do not love their neighbors as themselves. What a great shame and sorrow! Christians do not always have a spontaneous love for the Lord Jesus Christ. And it is for this reason they do not express a continual love for others!

How can we explain this failure? Is it that our heavenly Father has failed to provide for His children on earth? Certainly this is not the case. He has! But too many of us have not learned a simple lesson: *We must constantly renew our faith in God and in the power of His love in us through faith.*

Sometimes we try to stir up within our hearts a love toward God. Yet we become conscious that this cannot be done in our own strength. Faith comes first. We cannot awaken within ourselves the slightest love for God without faith. Oh, Christian, believe that the love of God will work in your heart as a vital power, enabling you to love your neighbors. True faith creates a total dependence upon God. Believe that His love will rest on you and abide in you. God will teach you how to love Him and others with His own love.

Learn the lesson of our text: "The love of God is shed abroad in our hearts by the Holy Spirit." The Holy Spirit will enable you to love God. The Holy Spirit will empower you to love your neighbors and even your enemies. Be assured of two things: (1) In your own strength you cannot love God or your neighbors. (2) The Holy Spirit within you seeks to fill you with the spirit of love.

Each morning, commit yourself into the keeping of the Holy Spirit. Pray this prayer: "Grant me the assurance that you will pour forth the love of Jesus into my own heart. Let the love of Christ stream forth to all those around me!"

The Practice of Christian Love

Christian love flows from the Holy Spirit, who influences our hearts. True Christian love arises toward God and others from the breathing of the Holy Spirit. The Spirit of God is the spirit of love. When the Holy Spirit enters our souls, love enters with Him. God is love. The person who has God dwelling in him by His Spirit also has God's love dwelling within him. The nature of the Holy Spirit is love. By communicating himself to Christians in His own nature, God fills their hearts with divine charity. Therefore, we find that Christians are partakers of the divine nature. Christian love is called the "love in the Spirit" and "love of the Spirit" (see Col. 1:8 and Rom. 15:30). The Holy Spirit infuses love for God. By the indwelling Holy Spirit, our souls abide in love for God and others (see Rom. 5:5 and 1 John 3:23, 24; 4:12, 13).

In conversion, the Holy Spirit renews our hearts by giving us a divine attitude. From this divine attitude, love flows out for both God and others. When we love God and others with a truly Christian love, we love them from the same motive. When God is rightly loved, He is loved for *who* He is, for His excellence, the beauty of His nature, and the holiness of His character. And it is for His holiness' sake that we love God and our fellow Christians. Again, love to God is the foundation of gracious love for others. We love some people because they are in some respect like God: they possess His nature and spiritual image. We love others simply because they are His children. And we must love still others simply because His mercy is offered to them.

Prayer

Dear Heavenly Father, teach me that I must totally depend upon you for all things, even my love for you and for my fellowman. I surely do not love you as I ought apart from your indwelling Holy Spirit, the Spirit of love. When I reflect upon all that you have done for me, I marvel that love does not spontaneously leap from my heart. Love is always the fruit of your Spirit. I thank you that this is so. It reminds me that no good will ever come forth from me unaided by you. This reminder will drive me to rely upon you continually for everything that I do, especially for the love that I want to share more perfectly with you and others, for Jesus' sake. Amen.

We are more than conquerors through him that loved us.

Rom. 8:37

6

The Power of Love

In these days of unrest and resurgence of racism and discrimination, we need above all to discover a new and living experience of the love of God. Let us anchor our hope in the thought "God is love." God rules and guides the world by the power of an undying, persistent love, working through the hearts, spirits and wills of people wholly yielded to Him and His service. He waits for us to open our hearts to Him so that He can fill us with love and courage to witness for Him.

When Christ's kingdom is manifested and His reign of love on earth is obvious, God's purpose has been achieved. Christ died in order to establish a kingdom of love on earth. While He was on earth, He influenced the world through His great serving, suffering love. He saw the possibility of redemption in the hearts of the most sinful and downcast. He knew that men's hearts could not forever resist the steady, continuous influence of love. Unbounded faith in the fire and fervor of God's love will enable us to expect and to do the impossible.

Argument or reproach will not overcome the spirit of hatred and bitterness. Only the omnipotent love of God will be the victor. As His children, we must learn to accept His love, not only for ourselves, but also for others. If we, who call ourselves "believers," will yield ourselves unreservedly to God for Him to work through us, then faith through love will prevail. Love as the greatest power in the world will prepare us for communion with God and intercession for others in prayer. Love will incline us to a life of unselfish service among our fellowmen. Examine your life. As a servant of All-Powerful Love, pray for its effect upon those around you.

The Practice of Christian Love

Contention is a spoiler of true Christianity. The Scriptures say, "Where envying and strife is, there is confusion and every evil work" (James 3:16). And so we find from experience. Whenever contention enters, it prevents the flow of Christian faith. Contention seems to chill and deaden faith. What flourishes instead is evil.

Contention directly opposes the essential and distinguishing marks of true Christianity: love and peace. Love cannot flourish in the midst of strife and contention among believers. Love and contention cannot live together.

We must diligently guard ourselves against envy, malice and every kind of bitterness toward others. These things are the exact reverse of the real essence of Christianity. We must suppress the first stirrings of ill will, bitterness and envy, or any attitude that leads in that direction. We must guard against everything that tends to overthrow, corrupt or undermine the spirit of love. Since unity is the principle of a truly Christian love, that which hinders love for others will hinder love for God. An envious, malicious, cold and hard-hearted Christian is the greatest absurdity and contradiction!

Since love is the attitude and spirit of the Christian, should we wonder that Christianity requires us to love our enemies, even the worst of them? In the gospel, we have set before us the love of God and Christ for their enemies. Should we wonder that we are required to love our enemies, bless them, do good to them and pray for them? Jesus declared that we must "be the children of [our] Father which is in heaven: for he maketh his sun to rise on the evil and on the good, and sendeth rain on the just and on the unjust" (Matt. 5:45).

The spirit of love is an amiable spirit, the very spirit of Jesus Christ. Harmony among the brethren brings joy and contentment; and love of our enemies makes us at peace with the world. Both reason and Scripture teach us that "happy is the man that findeth wisdom" and "her ways are ways of pleasantness, and all her paths are peace" (Prov. 3:13, 17).

Prayer

Dear Heavenly Father, I find it difficult to love my enemies when they are also your enemies. Too often I am inclined to pray for justice instead of mercy. Help me to manifest your love for them, even though I do not condone their actions, nor stand by and allow them to wreak havoc in your kingdom. When I must stand for the truth, help me to do so with the loving Spirit of your Son who gave His life that His enemies might be saved. I, too, was once your enemy, but I am saved by grace. Help me to share the message of saving grace to all who need to know your love. In Jesus' name. Amen.

By this shall all men know that ye are my disciples, if ye have love one to another.

John 13:35

7

The Sign of a True Church

We have been taught that the true Church is where God's Word is rightly preached and the holy sacraments are dispensed as instituted by Christ. Christ himself took a much broader view. To Him the distinguishing mark of His Church was not what her ministers taught and performed, but if His followers truly loved one another.

Please understand this important distinction. In God, love reaches its highest point. The culmination of His glory is love. Love at its fullest expression was in the man Christ Jesus on the cross. We owe everything to this love, because it is the power that moved Christ to die for us, and by which God highly exalted Him as Lord and Christ. Love is the power that broke our hearts, and love is the power that healed them. Love is the power through which Christ dwells in us and works in us—love can change our whole nature and enable us to surrender all to God. Love gives us the enabling to live a holy, joyous life, which in turn blesses others. As in a mirror, every Christian shows forth the love of God.

How seldom do Christians realize the truth of this! They

seek to love Christ and the brethren through human love, and of course they fail. Subsequently, they convince themselves of the impossibility of leading such a life, and they cease to desire it or pray for it. They do not understand the power at their disposal through God's own love, which is poured forth into our hearts by the Holy Spirit.

Oh, that this great truth might possess us: *the Holy Spirit dwelling within us sheds abroad in our hearts the love of God.* He will maintain this heavenly love from hour to hour. Through the loving work of the Holy Spirit, we shall be able to understand the word of Christ: "All things are possible to him that believeth" (Mark 9:23). We can love God and Christ with all our hearts. We can love our brethren, and even our enemies, while love flows from us as a stream of living water through the Holy Spirit.

The Practice of Christian Love

We have great reason to bless God and live to His glory, because we have received the influence of the Holy Spirit who works grace in our hearts. Seriously consider the state of the godly and you cannot but be amazed at the wonderful grace bestowed upon them. When we read in the Scriptures of the great privilege conferred on the Virgin Mary, as the mother of our Lord, or the Apostle Paul, when he was caught up into the third heaven, or any of the disciples who walked and talked with Jesus in the flesh, we stand in awe. But what can compare with the privilege of being like Christ and having His love in our hearts?

If you have the love of Christ in your heart, consider what great favor God has bestowed upon you. Consider how great your debt to glorify Him for the work His grace has wrought in you. He purchased this blessing for you with the blood of His own Son, and sealed it to your soul by His Holy Spirit.

Consider how highly He has advanced and exalted you. Will you be diligent to live and work for Him?

Some will dishonor Christ by neglecting the gift that is in them. Some will not give Him their whole heart, pursuing instead the pleasures of this world. Guard against a worldly or proud disposition that might lead you away from God who has been so long-suffering with you. Will you turn from a Savior who has purchased such blessings for you? Or will you inquire every day: "What shall I render unto the Lord for all his benefits toward me" (Ps. 116:12)? What more could God have done for you than He has already done?

Ask yourself these questions: How much have I done for God? How much have I done for self? How has His divine love inclined me to live for God and Christ and for the extension of His kingdom? Let us show our sense of privilege by the exercise of love—love toward God in obedience, submission, honor and worship; and love toward our neighbor in meekness, empathy, humility, generosity and doing good at every opportunity.

Prayer

Dear Heavenly Father, too often the mark of a true Christian is not upon me because I do not allow your love to flow through me to others. Too often this love is not present in churches because of strife, envy, jealousy and a party or denominational spirit. Forgive me when I have not shown to the world that a right belief and a right relationship with you through Jesus Christ brings forth love to others. Create in your Church and in me a desire to love as you love. Fulfill the longing of our hearts through your indwelling Holy Spirit of love, for Jesus' sake and those who need to know you. Amen.

For we ourselves also were sometimes foolish, disobedient, deceived, serving divers lusts and pleasures, living in malice and envy, hateful, and hating one another.

Titus 3:3

8

Racial Hatred

What a dark picture of human nature and society the Bible paints! Where does such a sad condition of things come from, worse even than we see among the animals? The answer is sin.

Just think how Cain, the first child born on earth, born of man whom God had created, murdered his own brother Abel. He came under the power of the devil, who "was a murderer from the beginning" (John 8:44).

In the time of Noah, "God saw that the wickedness of man was great in the earth, and that every imagination of the thoughts of his heart was only evil continually" (Gen. 6:5). No wonder He destroyed mankind by a flood. Yet soon after the flood there were signs that man was still under the power of sin. Man's love of his own people, implanted in his heart by God, soon changed to hatred of other peoples. Pride in one's own country and race became the root of race hatred, war, and bloodshed.

Note how in South Africa God has placed the two races side by side, as though in a school, to test the power of Christian love to overcome race hatred, and to prove that "in the new creature there is neither Greek nor Jew, circumcision nor uncircumcision, Barbarian, Scythian, bond nor free: but Christ is all, and in all" (Col. 3:11).

The Church of Christ and her ministers must preach and proclaim the love of God and prove its might to change racial hatred into brotherly love! God has abundant power to bring this to pass.

Pray for yourself and your brethren that you may not make the Word of God of none effect by your unbelief! Oh, God, make known to us your love in heavenly power and let it take full possession of our lives!

The Practice of Christian Love

How absurd to think that anything could make up for our not doing all that God requires. Love must have its seat in our hearts. All that is saving and distinguishing as a mark of true Christian character consists in love. The love of which our Savior speaks is the sum of all that the two tables of the Law require. The apostle says that love fulfills the Law. Do you think that you can make up for your lack of love for God and others when, by withholding love, you in effect withhold the sum total of all that God requires of you?

How absurd to suppose that you can make up for not doing something that God requires by doing something else that He requires. We cannot make up for one debt by paying another. It is even more absurd to suppose that you can make up for the whole debt by paying nothing at all and by continuing to withhold all that He requires. God requires us to do everything from our hearts. If we would like to have any external offering accepted, we must first give our hearts to Him.

To pretend you respect and love God, when this is not felt in your heart, is to presume you can deceive God!—He who knows all hearts and minds from the inside out. In the desert, Israel did "flatter him with their mouth, and they lied unto him with their tongues" (Ps. 78:36). Surely it is absurd for you to think that by flattery and guile you can make up for a lack of sincere respect, or that by falsehood and lying you can make up for lack of truth.

How ridiculous it would be if a wife thought that by giving her affections to another man, she could make up for her lack of love for her husband. How absurd for her to suppose that by sin and guilt of adultery, she could make up for her lack of faithfulness. How absurd for you to think that by loving God, or by any other so-called religious act, you can make up for your lack of love for your brethren, or for your enemies. A cup of cold water given to another in sincere love is worth far more in God's sight than giving, without love, all of your goods to feed the poor.

Prayer

Dear Heavenly Father, please bring to my attention any lack of love in my life or any act of love left undone. Where I lack love, fill me with your Spirit of love. Help me in a practical way to apply love in every relationship—whether with someone of another race or religion, or with a friend or enemy. Help me to love in a genuine way those who are opposed to you and your truth that I might win them for Jesus Christ whose love for them knows no limit. Amen.

Ye have heard that it hath been said: thou shalt love thy neighbor, and hate thine enemy.

Matt. 5:43

9

Love Your Enemies

In Christ's day, the Jewish rabbis taught people they could hate their enemies. They believed they had a right to teach this because of Lev. 19:17–18: "Thou shalt not hate thy brother in thine heart; thou shalt . . . not bear any grudge against the children of thy people; but thou shalt love thy neighbor as thyself." From these verses they argued that God had forbidden them to hate their own people; yet, they could hate their enemies. In contrast to this our Lord said, "Love your enemies, bless them that curse you" (Matt. 5:44).

Too often professing Christians follow the example of the Jewish teachers! For some believers, the command of our Lord is too strict and narrow. They have not yielded themselves to God in obedience to the new commandment to love their neighbors as themselves—even when that neighbor is an enemy. They do not believe that it is possible to love those who hate and curse them.

Again, we are faced with the issue of God's perfect love flowing through us or our own human love doing the job. Of course, only God's love is sufficient for the task.

When I was a minister in Cape Town, I met a German deaconess who was working with the English Church at

Woodstock. She had a class every evening for ten to twelve people who were preparing for admission to the church. One evening she spoke about loving our enemies. She asked one person if his people had enemies. "Oh yes!" he replied. "Who are they?" she asked. "The Fingoes." (The Kaffirs count the Fingoes as dogs.) She asked the man if he could love a Fingo. His answer was quite decided: "Me no love Fingo. Me no love Fingo." His reply was an indisputable fact. There could be no question about it. He could not love a Fingo. She told him that if he could not love his enemies, then he could not go to communion. He went home very thoughtful.

The next evening he attended class but was very downcast. She asked him again if he could love Fingoes. But still he had only one answer: "Me no love Fingo." He was not received into the church with the others, but he continued to attend class. He was always in earnest and evidently struggling.

One evening he appeared with a bright shining face and announced: "Me *now* love Fingo!" He had prayed continually about it, and God had heard his prayer.

You will discover that there is only one way to love your enemies. You must love them by the love of Christ. You will find the love of Christ if you seek it in prayer.

The Practice of Christian Love

The Apostle Paul declared: "Charity suffereth long, and is kind" (1 Cor. 13:4). Charity, or a truly Christian spirit, will incline us meekly to bear the evil that we receive from others.

Meekness is an essential ingredient of the Christian spirit. Christ invites all who labor and are heavy-laden to come to Him for rest. He particularly mentions that they should come to *learn* of Him. Then He adds, "I am meek and lowly in heart" (Matt. 11:29). With respect to injuries we receive from others, meekness is called *long-suffering* in the Scriptures. Long-suffering is a manifestation, or fruit, of the Holy Spirit. "The fruit of the Spirit is love, joy, peace, long-suffering" (Gal. 5:22).

Loving God the Father and the Lord Jesus Christ disposes us to imitate them. Therefore, we will be disposed to the same long-suffering that they manifest. The long-suffering of God is very wonderfully manifested in His bearing innumerable injuries from mankind. Consider the wickedness in the world. If you consider how God continues its existence, showers countless mercies upon it, and extends natural blessings to all, then you shall perceive His long-suffering love. He offers mercy to sinners even while they are rebelling against Him. When we love Him and allow His love to flow through us, we will love our enemies.

Long-suffering and humility are always found together. Contrarily, pride and self-conceit breed bitterness and resentment, an unforgiving and revengeful spirit. Let us endeavor under all injuries to preserve a calm and quiet spirit, allowing the manifestation of the Spirit's long-suffering. We must be ready to suffer unjustly ourselves, rather than stir up strife and contention.

Prayer

Dear Heavenly Father, I have not loved my enemies as I ought to have loved them. I have not imitated you in my relationship with them. Too quickly I have prayed for your judgment instead of your grace to come upon them. Help me to remember that today I live under your mercy and grace—I am no longer estranged from you simply because of your grace. Help me to extend your mercy and long-suffering to my enemies, and open the door for me to share the saving gospel of your Son with them. For the sake of His kingdom. Amen.

I will forgive their iniquity, and I will remember their sin no more.

Jer. 31:34

10

To Forgive but Not to Forget

At the unveiling of the Women's Monument at Bloemfontein in 1913, I happened to be sitting in the front row on the platform at the foot of the monument. After a while the sun became very hot. Suddenly, I noticed that someone behind me was holding an umbrella over my head. When the speaker had finished, I asked my nephew: "Who is so friendly as to hold an umbrella over my head?" He replied, "General de Wet." I was surprised and turned around and thanked him heartily. Afterward, my nephew told me that the general had said, "But I would gladly have paid for the privilege of doing it." I thought, *what a generous nature to speak in that way!*

Presently, General de Wet rose to give his address. I could agree with all that he said except his last words, which were "forgive—yes, but forget—never." When the ceremony was over, I shook hands with him again. From my heart I said to him, "You said, 'I can never forget.' Be careful to what that may lead."

Many people have allowed themselves to be deceived by

these words: "Forgive but not forget." On the farm, I have often seen a dog come into the house at the front door to seek coolness and shade. He would be driven out and the door was closed behind him. Then he would go around the house and come in through the back door. Think of the front door as "I will forgive." You *want* to put away all thought of hatred or ill-feeling. But like the dog circling the house and creeping in the back door ("I will never forget"), how quickly and quietly these evil thoughts return.

Many people trust in God's forgiving love. However, they do not remember that when God forgives He also forgets. He has said, "I will forgive their iniquity, and will remember their sins no more" (Jer. 31:34). And the Apostle Paul gives us this advice in Col. 3:13, "Forgiving one another . . . even as Christ forgave you, so also do ye."

The Practice of Christian Love

If you are not disposed to bear injuries meekly, then you are not equipped to live in this evil world. We do not dwell in a world of purity, innocence and love, but one that is fallen, corrupt, miserable and wicked. We live in a world under the dominion of sin. Here the devil has influence and dominion, and multitudes are possessed of his spirit. The principle of divine love that was once in the heart of man is extinguished and now reigns in only a few.

Not many have that spirit of faith in their hearts which leads to a life governed by the rules of justice and kindness toward others. The world is too much like that of which our Savior spoke: "I send you forth as sheep in the midst of wolves" (Matt. 10:16). Therefore, if you do not have a spirit of meekness, calmness, and long-suffering to bear offenses in such a world, then you will be miserable indeed.

If every injury and reproach, every malicious and unjust

deed ruffles your spirit, then you are in perpetual turmoil. Even unintentional remarks or deeds by your brothers in the Lord will disturb you if you are not dependent on the gentle, long-suffering of the Spirit of God.

Do not allow yourself to become angry at personal offenses. Do not allow bitter resentment to arise within you when you are misunderstood or neglected, as though some strange thing has happened to you. Remind yourself that this is part of the human condition. Offenses will come. How we respond to those offenses is the test of our faith and dependence upon the fruits of the Spirit in us.

Prayer

Dear Heavenly Father, thank you for sharing with me the secret of your own heart: the spirit of forgiveness. You have not required anything of me for which you have not also provided your enabling. Indeed, the character you want me to have is nothing less than your own character manifested through the sacrificial death of your Son for the forgiveness of sins. Help me to maintain your attitude toward personal injuries, so when I am hurt, I can respond with a love that may lead my enemies to salvation through faith in Jesus Christ. Amen.

And forgive us our sins; for we also forgive every one that is indebted to us.

Luke 11:4

11

As God Forgives

Forgiveness of sins is a great all-embracing gift of God. In His mercy, God sets the sinner free and receives him back into His love and favor. When we are forgiven, we have confidence toward God in prayer. We can be thankful every day of our lives because we are free and nothing stands between us and God. With the door open to communion with Him, God desires that we spend time with Him in His Word each day as people whose sins are forgiven. We need to live in the light of His countenance daily.

And God desires that this assurance affect our relationship with others. Those who are forgiven are free to forgive others. If it is difficult to forgive, we should consider how freely God has forgiven us of every offense toward Him.

How clearly and urgently our Lord speaks on this! In the Lord's Prayer He taught us to pray each day: "Forgive us our debts, as we forgive our debtors" (Matt. 6:12). And then Jesus says, "If ye forgive not men their trespasses, neither will your Father forgive your trespasses" (Matt. 6:15).

After His great promise recorded in Mark 11:25 come the words: "And when ye stand praying, forgive, if ye have aught against any." In Matt. 18:21, Peter asked, "Lord, how oft shall my brother sin against me, and I forgive him?" Our Lord answered, "Unto seventy times seven."

Remember the parable of the servant whose lord forgave him his debt but who would not show compassion on his fellow servant? His lord asked him, "Shouldest not thou also have had mercy on thy fellow servant, even as I had pity on thee?" And He was delivered to his tormentors. Our Lord warns: "So likewise shall my heavenly Father do also unto you, if ye from your hearts forgive not every one his brother their trespasses" (Matt. 18:35).

Remember these words daily: *As I need God's forgiveness each day, so let me be ready each day to forgive my brother.* God grant you grace to do it!

The Practice of Christian Love

When you are persecuted or injured, you will demonstrate the mark of true greatness if you maintain the spirit of Christian patience, meekness, and forgiveness. You will manifest excellence of temper, inward fortitude and strength, when you remain steady and forgiving in the midst of your tormentors. Of course, this inward strength is not your own, but the power of the Spirit of Love in you. Solomon said, "He that is slow to anger is better than the mighty: and he that ruleth his spirit than he that taketh a city" (Prov. 16:32). The demonstration of true Christian character is more powerful than the influence of the greatest of men.

Not drawing on the resources available to them, some Christians are easily disturbed and lose their repose through the reproaches and ill treatment of others. They can be compared to small streams of water that are much disturbed by the unevenness of their course and obstacles in the path. They also make a great deal of noise as they pass over the roughness. However, great and mighty streams pass over the same obstacles calmly and quietly without a ripple on the surface to show they are disturbed.

If you possess your soul in such a way that when others harm and injure you, you can, nevertheless, remain calm and in goodwill toward them, forgiving them from the heart, then you manifest a godlike spirit. Such a meek, quiet, and long-suffering spirit displays the greatness of our God, and we glorify Him through our behavior. So says the Apostle James: "Who is a wise man and endued with knowledge among you? let him show out of a good conversation his works with meekness of wisdom" (James 3:13).

If you are highly apt to resent ill treatment or to be greatly angered when you are not honored, then you are spoken of in the Scriptures as possessing a little and foolish spirit. On the other hand, if you maintain a meek spirit, then you are expressly spoken of in the Scriptures as having an honorable spirit: "It is an honor for a man to cease from strife" (Prov. 20:3). How can you be at peace with anyone you will not forgive?

Prayer

Dear Heavenly Father, help me to forgive others as you have forgiven me. Help me to bear with any insults and injuries in calmness of spirit. Where I must stand and defend the truth, help me to do so with a nobility of purpose that indicates my love and concern for both you and my fellowman. Help me to distinguish major issues in life from the minor annoyances that I should expect from living in this world and from battling all the foes of goodness. Help me to live according to the direction of your Holy Spirit for the sake of the establishment of your kingdom and Jesus' sake. Amen.

The greatest of these is love.

1 Cor. 13:13

12

The Preaching of Love

During the Boer War, when there was much unrest in the country, a certain minister asked his brother-minister, who was a leader in the Church, to do his best to calm the minds of those around him. He answered: "I have enough trouble with myself. My own mind is unsettled. How can I quiet others?" If the preaching of love were revived, more than one minister would have to say: "I lack so much love in my own heart; how can I teach others?"

Yet there is a remedy. Let me tell you what I have learned from John Wesley. During the first fourteen years of his ministry, he had no insight into what a free and full salvation by faith meant. After he had been convicted of the sin of unbelief, by means of a conversation with one of the Moravian brethren, he began to preach with such power that many were converted. But he felt that it was too much a matter of intellect. He had not yet experienced the full joy and love that the Moravian possessed. He asked the brother what he should do. He answered: "Preach it because you believe that is what God's Word teaches. You will soon find what you are seeking. And then you will preach it because you possess it."

This has been my own experience. Often in preaching or in writing I have asked myself: *But do you possess what you preach to others?* And I have followed the advice: *Preach it because you believe it to be the teaching of God's Word and heartily desire it. Preach the truth by faith, and the experience will follow.*

Let the minister who feels motivated to preach about love not hesitate to do so. He will soon be able to preach about love because he himself has received that which he commends.

The Practice of Christian Love

The Scriptures teach that we will be dealt with by God hereafter according to the way we deal with others here. Thus, "with the merciful thou wilt show thyself merciful; with an upright man thou wilt show thyself upright" (Ps. 18:25). And again, "with what judgment ye judge, ye shall be judged: and with what measure ye mete, it shall be measured to you again" (Matt. 7:2).

Faith, hope and love go together. Love believes all things and hopes all things. Love is greater than both, because the influence of love produces both faith and hope. They are linked together as a chain; therefore, if one link is broken the whole ceases to be effective. Where one of these fruits of the Spirit is lacking, all of them are lacking.

Where there is faith, there is love, hope and humility. Where there is love to God, there is trust in God, and a gracious hope, which also produces a holy fear of God. And where there is love to God, there is a gracious love for others.

Hence, the Apostle John wrote, "If a man say, I love God, and hateth his brother, he is a liar" (1 John 4:20).

The Christian graces depend upon one another. To deny one would deny the other, just as to deny the cause would deny the effect. Faith promotes love, and love is the most effective ingredient in a living faith. Love depends on faith, for you cannot love God unless you look upon Him in genuine faith that He is the One true Living God. Love enlarges and promotes faith because we are more apt to believe and give credit to those we love than those we do not love. Faith begets hope because faith sees and trusts in God's sufficiency to bestow blessings and be faithful to fulfill His promises. All gracious hope rests on faith. And hope encourages and draws forth acts of faith. So love tends to hope, for the spirit of love is the spirit of a child, which is a spirit of confidence and hope.

True and genuine hope greatly promotes love. When a Christian hopes most in God and in His eternal blessings, love is the natural response. As the Apostle Paul wrote, "Tribulation worketh patience; and patience, experience; and experience, hope; and hope maketh not ashamed: because the love of God is shed abroad in our hearts" (Rom. 5:3–5).

Prayer

Dear Heavenly Father, thank you for the wisdom and faithfulness of such men as Jonathan Edwards, Andrew Murray and John Wesley. Thank you for the advice of the unknown Moravian brother who made a difference in the ministry of Wesley and others who followed the simple advice he gave. May I experience the truth of your Word in a personal way and declare it faithfully as these men did. Help me to know in my heart what I know in my head that I might preach, teach, and share the gospel with loving power in Jesus' holy name. Amen.

I exhort therefore, that, first of all, supplications, prayers, intercessions, and giving of thanks, be made for all men; for kings, and for all that are in authority, that we may lead a quiet and peaceable life in all godliness and honesty.

1 Tim. 2:1, 2

13
The Two Leaders

Before the procession took place at the unveiling of the Women's Monument at Bloemfontein, I spoke a few words in the Dutch Church about the suffering, praying, all-conquering love of these women who prayed earnestly that God would keep them from hatred or lack of love toward their enemies. I expressed the hope that this prayerful love might be ours, and that nothing might be done to disturb the feeling of peace and unity. I said that there were some who feared disunity between the two races in the country and also between those who were fellow countrymen. Not long after, we heard that there had been a breach between the leaders of the two parties.

In view of this division, I felt compelled to write an article on the question: "For whom do you pray?" Someone wrote and answered: "I pray for the man at the head of the government, who, under God's guidance as general of the burghers in the war, has not become the leader of all South Africa." And another responded: "I pray especially for the man who has been instrumental in bringing the interests of his people to the forefront." How sad it would be if we came into God's presence divided into two camps, praying one against the other! No, we must pray for *all* leaders and for *all* who are in authority. As leaders of the people, their influence for good or evil is significant. Their hearts are in God's hands and He can turn them whithersoever He wills—as King Solomon declared, "The king's heart is in the hand of the Lord, as the rivers of water: he turneth it whithersoever he will" (Prov. 21:1).

Let our prayers ascend to God in all sincerity, and He will hear and grant that which is good for everyone. Let us pray: "Lord, the hearts of all rulers are in Thy hands; teach them to do Thy will."

The Practice of Christian Love

What a great honor to be made an instrument of good in the world. When we fill our lives with doing the will of God, He often puts the high honor upon us of making us a blessing to the world—an honor such as He placed on Abraham when He said, "I will bless thee, and make thy name great; and thou shalt be a blessing" (Gen. 12:2).

Eastern kings and governors used to assume for themselves the title of "Benefactor." Benefactors were the doers of good; so, this title was the most honorable they could think of to call themselves: "And he [Jesus] said unto them, The kings of the Gentiles exercise lordship over them; and they that exercise authority upon them are called benefactors" (Luke 22:25).

Unfortunately, it was a common thing in heathen lands, when those who had done a great deal of good in their lifetime were dead, for the people to reckon them as gods and build temples to their honor to worship them. So far as God makes people the instruments of doing good to others, He makes them like the heavenly bodies—the sun, moon and stars that bless the world by shedding their light. He makes them like the angels, who are ministering spirits to others for their good. Yes, He makes them like himself, the great fountain of all good who is forever pouring down His blessings on all mankind.

The spirit of Christian love is opposed to a selfish spirit and disposes people to be public-spirited. A man of a right spirit is not a man of narrow and private views, but is greatly interested and concerned for the good of the community to which he belongs and the true welfare of society. God commanded the Jews who were carried away captive to Babylon to seek the good of that city, though it was not their native place but the city of their captivity: "Seek the peace of the city whither I have caused you to be carried away captives, and pray unto the Lord for it" (Jer. 29:7). A person of a truly Christian spirit will be earnest for the good of his country and work for its improvement.

Of such a charitable spirit was Paul, who was so concerned for the welfare of all, both Jews and Gentiles, that he was willing to become as they were if possibly he might save some (see 1 Cor. 9:19–23).

Prayer

Dear Jesus, you lived, loved, and died for all nations. Help me to see beyond the boundaries of class, race or party, and work for the welfare of all mankind. Keep me from any unbiblical, narrow views that would hinder my effectiveness to reach out, to seek and to save those who are lost without the saving knowledge of you. Amen.

Seeing ye have purified your souls in obeying the truth through the Spirit, unto unfeigned love of the brethren, see that ye love one another with a pure heart fervently.

1 Pet. 1:22

14
Unfeigned Love of the Brethren

In the beginning of his letter, Peter expressed a wonderful truth about our love to Christ: "Whom having not seen, ye love; in whom, though now you see him not, yet believing, ye rejoice with joy unspeakable and full of glory" (1 Pet. 1:8). This was the fruit of the Spirit.

In our text he speaks of "the love of the brethren." "Ye have purified your souls in obeying the truth through the Spirit, unto unfeigned love of the brethren." In the days of the early church, new converts clearly understood that in confessing Christ, they also promised unfeigned love to the brethren. So Peter continues: "See that ye love one another with a pure heart fervently." Unfeigned, fervent love through the Spirit should be the chief sign of a true conversion.

See how much stress Peter placed on this point in the next three chapters of his letter. In 2:17, he returned to the subject: "Love the brotherhood. Fear God. Honor the king." In 3:8, he wrote: "Finally, be ye all of one mind, compassionate, having compassion one of another, love as brethren, be pitiful, be courteous." All of these are signs that the life of God is in the soul. Then he commended in 4:7, 8, "Watch unto prayer. And above all things have fervent charity among yourselves; for charity [love] shall cover the multitude of sins." Unfeigned, fervent love of the brethren was the indispensable sign of true godliness.

God's Word is a mirror into which the Church, including each individual member, must look to see whether we are truly Christian, showing by our conduct that we take God's Word as our rule of life. If our hearts condemn us, we must turn at once to God, confessing our sin (see 1 John 3:20, 21). Let us believe that the Spirit of Love does indeed dwell in us and will shed abroad God's love in our hearts and purify us from all hatred and selfishness and restore the image of Christ within us. Let us not rest content until we have surrendered ourselves wholly to God that His Spirit of Love may reign and rule within us.

The Practice of Christian Love

Freely do good to others. Do to them as you would have them do to you. When others show goodwill toward you, and are kind and ready to help when you are in need, you highly commend their attitude and conduct. If they freely suffer for you, bear your burdens, feel for you in your distresses, and are warmhearted toward you, you highly approve of their spirit and actions, do you not? You not only approve of them, but you seek occasions to speak well of them. You never think that they have exceeded their duty. If all of this is so noble and to be commended in others when you are the object, you ought to do the same for them and to everyone about you. What we thus approve in others, we should exemplify in our own conduct.

Consider how kind God has been to us, and how much good we daily benefit from His hand. Divine mercies are new to us every morning and fresh every evening: they are as ceaseless as our being. And still greater good things God has bestowed for our spiritual and eternal good. He has given us what is of more value than all the kingdoms of the earth—His only begotten and well-beloved Son, the greatest gift that He could bestow. And Christ has suffered great things and given himself to die for us—all freely, without promise or hope of reward.

God has truly done great things for those who are His children. How we love Him for delivering us from sin, justifying and sanctifying us, making us kings and priests unto God, and giving us a title "to an inheritance that is incorruptible, and undefiled, and that fadeth not away" (1 Pet. 1:4). Let us love others that they may experience this wonderful position in Christ.

Prayer

Dear Heavenly Father, thank you so much for the gift of your Son and the life I have through Him. Thank you so much for Christian brothers and sisters who have loved me and cared for me throughout the years without any hope of personal gain. Help me to love others fervently from the heart, and then help me to see and discover practical ways to love them in action. I pray this in Jesus' name, who is my greatest example. Amen.

The fruit of the Spirit is love.

Gal. 5:22

God hath given us the spirit of love.

2 Tim. 1:7

15
The Spirit of Love

The fruit of the Holy Spirit is love. Christian love does not consist in a mere knowledge of the divine love for us. Nor does Christian love consist in faith in God's love as revealed in our redemption. No, the matter goes far deeper. Our love originates from God's love shed abroad in our hearts by the Holy Spirit. God's love is more than an experience or feeling. The Spirit of Love takes possession of us. He directs, controls and inspires us. Christ's love becomes a heavenly life-power. He grants us a disposition that enables us to taste and know that God is good.

The Holy Spirit fills true Christians with the power of divine love; therefore, they can keep the commandments without difficulty. "This is the love of God, that we keep his commandments, and his commandments are not grievous" (1 John 5:3).

According to His promise, when God writes His Law in our hearts, the Law is summed up as love. Love governs the life of those wholly devoted to God. Love controls their thoughts and actions. Divine love in the heart of a Christian is like a sanctuary. From this sanctuary the Christian receives power to obey the inner law of love and to always live in the love of God. Holy love includes fellowship with God, union with Christ, and love to the brethren.

Now, how can we attain this experience? Through faith alone. The chief sign of faith in those who came to Christ for healing was their knowledge of their inability to help themselves. We must open our eyes and realize that the love of God has already been shed abroad in our hearts by His Spirit. We must realize that He enables us to keep His commandments and to love the brethren. As we acknowledge these facts, we must prayerfully bow in stillness before God. In this quietness, we must adore God and His love that has taken possession of our hearts until our faith can firmly say: "God has indeed given me the Spirit of Love in my heart. In the power of the Spirit, I can and will love God and my fellowman."

The Practice of Christian Love

Love to God inclines Christians to honor, worship, and adore Him. Love for God motivates them to heartily acknowledge His greatness, glory, and dominion. Love disposes them to obey God. As the servant who loves his master, and as the subject who loves his sovereign, the true Christian will be motivated to proper obedience and subjection to God.

Love motivates Christians to behave toward God as a child to his father. Amid difficulties, children resort to their father for help and put their trust in him. Naturally, in case of need or affliction we will go to the one we love for sympathy and help. God is more able and willing to help us than any other. When we love Him, we run to Him with every care.

Love for God leads us to trust His Word implicitly and to put our confidence in Him. We are not apt to suspect the honesty of those we call our friends. How much more will true love for God incline us to place absolute trust in His Word.

Love should dispose us to praise God for the mercies we receive from Him, just as we are grateful for any kindness we receive from those we love. Love will incline us to submit to the will of God, because we naturally desire that the will of those we love be done, and that they be pleased with us. Likewise, true affection for God will dispose our hearts to acknowledge His right to govern. Moreover, we will stoutly declare that He is worthy to govern over all. True affection for God will motivate us to submit to Him entirely in all things.

Love to God will motivate us to walk humbly before Him, and give Him His rightful place in all things. A true believer proclaims that God is worthy of exaltation, and from love he delights to cast himself at the feet of the Most High.

Prayer

Dear Heavenly Father, I do not deserve your love for me. I have grievously sinned against you and my fellowman. I have fallen short of your glory. Yet, your love for me is unchanging. Fill me afresh with your Holy Spirit that I may love you with the pure and holy love that I desire, and from that love do your will on earth. Amen.

And now abideth faith, hope, love, these three; but the greatest of these is love.

1 Cor. 13:13

16

A Song of Love

The thirteenth chapter of First Corinthians is wholly devoted to the praise of love. The first three verses speak of the absolute necessity of love as the chief motivation of our faith. "If I speak with the tongues of angels, if I have the gift of prophecy, if I have all faith, so as to remove mountains, and if I bestow all my goods on the poor, and if I give my body to be burned, but have not love," then, three times repeated, "I am become sounding brass. I am nothing. It profiteth me nothing." If I have not love, it all profits me nothing.

Then follows, in verses four through eight, fifteen things about love—what it is and what it is not. In this description one sentence sums up the whole nature of love: "It seeketh not her own." And again: "Love never faileth." Prophecies, tongues, and knowledge shall vanish away. Even faith and hope shall be changed into sight. But love abides to all eternity, as long as God endures. Love is the greatest thing in the world.

We should read this chapter more often than we do. We should commit this Song of Love to memory so that the great words are imprinted on our hearts: "Love seeketh not her own." Think over it and pray over it. "Love never faileth." Consider all that means. "The greatest of these is love." Let this love rule in your life.

God is love. "He that dwelleth in love dwelleth in God, and God in him" (1 John 4:16). Oh, Christian, are you living in a world that is uncharitable and selfish, or full of bitterness and hatred? Take refuge under the wings of this everlasting love. Let your heart be filled with it so that by God's almighty power, you may be a witness to the transforming power of love. Thus you will be a fountain of blessing to all around you.

Live each day in fellowship with the triune love of Father, Son and Holy Spirit, and you will learn the secret of how to love.

The Practice of Christian Love

To love ourselves is not unlawful. The law of God makes self-love a rule and measure by which our love to others should be regulated. Thus Christ commands, "Thou shalt love thy neighbor as thyself" (Matt. 19:19). He certainly supposes that we may and must love ourselves. He does not say that we are to love our neighbor *more than* ourselves but *as* ourselves. Since we are commanded to love our neighbor next to God, we should love ourselves with a love next to the love we have for God himself. Plainly, Christian love is not contrary to *all* self-love. If we hate ourselves, we despise what God has created and redeemed to be a vessel of His Spirit in the world.

Contrarily, selfishness is an inordinate self-love. In and of itself, self-love is not a result of the Fall, but is necessary and belongs to all intelligent beings. Saints and sinners alike love happiness and have an instinctive inclination to desire and seek it. When a person is converted and sanctified, his love for happiness is not diminished; it is regulated with respect to its exercise, influence, and the courses and objects it seeks.

Inordinate self-love is too great a love for self and confines happiness to oneself. Self-love, when it is inordinate, becomes a greater motivation in life than love for God or neighbor. Concern for one's own happiness may consume a person to the detriment of his soul and the well-being of his neighbor. In some respects wicked people do not love themselves enough—not as much as the godly do; for they do not love the path to their own welfare and happiness. In this sense we sometimes say of the wicked, "They hate themselves"; though in another sense they love themselves too much. Selfishness must be abandoned, and we must do all that we do from true love of God and our neighbor.

Prayer

Dear Heavenly Father, help me to have the proper balance of love in my life: love for you, love for my neighbor, and love for myself. Help me to judge rightly my actions, so that everything I do will be done to promote your happiness, my neighbor's happiness, and my own. Help me to avoid loving myself to the hurt of others, and help me to love myself enough to maintain a life that may be of service to all who have need, through your Son I pray. Amen.

If ye love me, keep my commandments.

John 14:15

17
The Obedience of Love

The Father loves the Son with a wonderful, never-ending love. Everything the Father is and has He gave to the Son. The Son responded to this love by giving all to the Father. Cost what it might, He kept the Father's commandments and abided in His love.

In His great love to us, Christ sacrificed all. His life and death were wholly at our service. He asks from us that which is only reasonable, that we should keep His commandments out of love. Read John 14:15, 21, and 23. Notice how the words "keep my commandments" or "keep my words" are repeated three times, together with the great promise that follows. Read John 15:7, 10, and 14, and notice how these verses speak three times of the rich blessings connected with the keeping of the commandments.

"If ye love me, keep my commandments." This precept loses its power when Christians say: "It is quite impossible; I cannot always keep His commandments." Conscience is quieted, and the commands are not kept. Yet our Lord really intended that the Christian keep His commands; for in the last night with His disciples, Jesus promised them a new life in which the power of the Spirit would enable them to live a life of obedience.

Though while on earth man remains in the flesh, he need not be controlled by his flesh. "In me, (that is, in my flesh,) dwelleth no good thing" (Rom. 7:18). The Holy Spirit is the power of God that works within me both to will and to do, and so prevents the flesh from controlling the life. Think of the text in Heb. 13:20, 21: "The God of peace . . . make you perfect in every good work to do his will, working in you that which is well-pleasing in his sight, through Jesus Christ."

Oh, brother, these are no mere idle words: "If ye love me, keep my commandments," and "My Father will love him, and we will make our abode with him." Believe that the Holy Spirit will cause the love of Christ to work in your heart in such power that you will be able to abide in the love of Jesus the whole day and keep His words with great joy. Then you will understand the saying: "This is the love of God, that we keep his commandments: and his commandments are not grievous" (1 John 5:3). Only believe that the Holy Spirit will endue you with power to live this life of perfect love.

The Practice of Christian Love

Humility inclines us to distrust our *selves* and depend only upon God. The proud person has a high opinion of his own wisdom or strength or righteousness and is inordinately self-confident. The humble rely upon God and delight to cast themselves wholly on Him as their refuge, righteousness, and strength.

The humble person will renounce all the glory of the good he has or does and give it all to God. If there is anything good in him or any good done by him, he is not disposed to glorify himself or boast about it before God. He will say with the Psalmist, "Not unto us, O Lord, not unto us, but unto thy name give glory, for thy mercy, and thy truth's sake" (Ps. 115:1). The disposition of the humble person is to wholly submit himself to God. His heart is not opposed to a full and absolute subjection to the divine will, but is inclined to it. He is content to be subject to the commands and laws of God, for he sees it is right and good that the creature be subject to His Creator. He wants to give God the honor that belongs to Him, and that is to reign over him and subject him to certain laws and commands that are designed for his own best interests.

Humility tends to prevent an inordinate aspiring to wealth or position—in short, ambitious behavior among people. A humble person is content with such a situation among others as God is pleased to allot to him and is not greedy for honor. Nor does he try to appear uppermost and exalted above his neighbors. He acts on the principle of that saying of the prophet, "Seekest thou great things for thyself? seek them not" (Jer. 45:5). Follow the command of the Apostle Paul: "Be of the same mind one toward another. Mind not high things, but condescend to men of low estate. Be not wise in your own conceits" (Rom. 12:16).

Prayer

Dear Holy Spirit of God, come into my life and empower me to do the will of my heavenly Father even as His Only Son obeyed Him. Keep me from trusting in myself, thinking that I can obey the Law of Love in my own power, instead of relying upon your love within me. Grant me the wisdom to know how to apply the Word of Truth in every situation, living humbly before you and before men. In Jesus' name. Amen.

Be ye therefore sober, and watch unto prayer. And above all things have fervent love among yourselves.

1 Pet. 4:7, 8

18
Love and Prayer

In our text, watching unto prayer and fervent love are closely linked. If you pray only for yourself, you will not find it easy to maintain a right attitude toward God. But when your heart is filled with fervent love to others, prayer will continually rise to God for those whom you love, and even for those with whom you do not agree.

There would be a great lack in this book on Christian love if we neglected to indicate what an important place prayer holds in the life of love. If you wish your love to grow and increase, you must deny yourself even in prayer, praying earnestly for God's children and His Church. And if you would *increase in prayerfulness,* give yourself in fervent love to the service of those around you, helping to bear their burdens.

What a great need there is for earnest, powerful intercessors! Let those who complain that there is so little love among Christians acknowledge that one of the chief signs of a lack of love is perhaps in themselves—that of infrequent prayer for their brethren. I am deeply convinced that God desires His children, as members of one body, to present themselves each day before the throne of grace to pray for an outpouring of the power of the Spirit upon all believers. Union is strength. This is true in regard to the kingdom of heaven. Real spiritual unity will help us to forget ourselves, to live wholly for God and our fellowmen. And the word of Peter will be applied to our lives: "watching in prayer—fervent in love."

There can be no surer way of growing in the Spirit of Love than by uniting daily at the throne of grace and finding our joy and life in the oneness of Spirit with the whole body of Christ. Let this book on love be also a book on prayer. As we meditate on love to one another, we shall be constrained to have fellowship with God. And we shall attain this, not by reading or thinking, but by communion with the Father and with the Lord Jesus through the Holy Spirit. Love compels us to pray. The love of God is bestowed upon believing prayer.

The Practice of Christian Love

Those who have the spirit of charity or Christian love have a spirit to seek the good of their fellowmen in prayer and in many other practical ways. Thus the Apostle Paul commands, "Look not every man on his own things, but every man also on the things of others" (Phil. 2:4). If we have a Christian spirit, we shall desire and seek their salvation, spiritual welfare and happiness. We shall want them to glorify and enjoy God forever with us.

The Christian spirit will also dispose us to desire and seek the temporal prosperity of others, as the apostle wrote: "Let no man seek his own, but every man another's wealth" (1 Cor. 10:24). We should seek to promote their pleasure and their profit. Again the apostle said, "Even as I please all men in all things, not seeking mine own profit, but the profit of many, that they may be saved" (1 Cor. 10:33). And again,

"Let every one of us please his neighbor for his good to edification" (Rom. 15:2).

The Christian spirit is a sympathizing and merciful spirit. Christians are inclined to consider not only their own difficulties but also the burdens and afflictions of others. They will ponder the difficulties of their circumstances and regard the case of those who are in troubles similar to their own. A selfish person is ready to make much of his afflictions, as if his sufferings were greater than those of anyone else. If he is not suffering, he does not think he is called to spare his possessions to help others.

A selfish person is not apt to see the needs of others but rather to overlook them. He can hardly be persuaded to feel for those who are suffering nor pray for anyone but himself. But a Christian is prone to see the afflictions of others, be filled with concern for them, help them and take delight in supplying their needs and relieving their problems whether material or spiritual.

Prayer

Dear Heavenly Father, help me to intercede more for the needs of others, specifically mentioning their needs whether spiritual or physical. Help me to recognize ways I can meet their needs from the resources you have given me. Help me to find ways of bringing Christians together to pray and work as one body for the glory of your name and the well-being of your people, in Jesus' name. Amen.

The Lord thy God will circumcise thine heart . . . to love the Lord thy God with all thine heart, and with all thy soul.

Deut. 30:6

19

The First and Great Commandment

God greatly desires our love. The nature of all love is to long to be acceptable and to meet with response. Yes, God longs with a never-ending, fervent desire to have our love, the love of our whole heart.

But how can we love God with our whole heart? In the same way that we receive salvation—through faith alone. Paul says: "I live through the faith of the Son of God, who loved me" (Gal. 2:20). When we take the time to wait upon God and remember the burning desire with which He sought to win our love—through the gift of His Son—we shall be able to realize that God has a strong and never-ceasing longing for the love of our hearts.

Our hearts are blind and dark, and we are inclined to forget that God longs each day for the love of His children. If I once begin to believe it, I shall feel constrained to tarry before God and ask Him to let His light shine into my heart. Just as the sun is willing to give me its light and heat, if I will receive them, God is a thousand times more willing to give me the light and glow of His love.

In the Old Testament God gave us the promise of the new covenant: "From all your filthiness, and all your idols, will I cleanse you. A new heart also will I give you, and a new spirit will I put within you" (Ezek. 36:25, 26). He gave His Son to die for us in order to win our love. *Take time, oh, my soul, to grasp this and wait silently upon God and become strong in the assurance of faith.* God, who longs for my love, is almighty. He will shed abroad His love in my heart through the Holy Spirit now dwelling within me.

Oh, that we could understand that there is nothing on earth to be compared to this experience! Shall I not take time each day to give God His desire and believe Him for the love He alone can give? God, who so greatly longs for my love, will work within me by His Spirit, granting the desire to love Him with my whole heart, and enabling me to prove my love by keeping His commandments.

O Lord, I bow before Thee; fulfill my longing desire, which is also Thy desire, that my heart may be filled with Thy love.

The Practice of Christian Love

Consider what the Scriptures teach us about the nature of the love to God: *Those who truly love God wholly devote themselves to Him and His service.* We are taught this as the summation of the Ten Commandments: "Thou shalt love the Lord thy God with all thy heart, and with all thy soul, and with all thy mind, and with all thy strength" (Mark 12:30). The whole being is devoted to God in love: the heart, the soul, the mind, the strength—all powers and faculties.

Nothing is held in reserve; true love for God enables one to do this. The love principle is far above the selfish principle. When a person is devoted wholly to God, love has conquered self.

Those who have true love to God love Him *as God.* They love Him *as the Supreme Good.* The principle of selfishness sets up self in place of God and makes an idol of self. The one that we regard supremely, we devote all to. If self is idolized, we devote all our time and energies to self. Contrarily, if we love God for who He truly is, we devote all to Him.

Christian love is in complete contradiction to a selfish spirit. Christians must be drawn to God and motivated by the Holy Spirit of love to devote all they have and are to the glory of God the Father and His Son, Jesus Christ. Pray for His Spirit to fill you with such love that you will have no room for selfishness and self-seeking, but can live totally for the service of the kingdom of God.

Prayer

Dear Heavenly Father, I come before you now and declare my love for you with my whole heart, mind, soul and strength; use me as you see fit. I am not worthy to be your servant, but your great love enables me to serve as I ought. Fill me with your Spirit, and reveal to me where there may still be a selfish attitude, and remove it from me that I might live wholly for you with the abilities and gifts you have bestowed. In Jesus' name. Amen.

If ye fulfill the royal law according to the scripture, Thou shalt love thy neighbor as thyself, ye do well.

James 2:8

20
The Royal Law of Love

When one of the Pharisees, a lawyer, asked our Lord, "Master, which is the great commandment in the law?" Jesus answered, "Thou shalt love the Lord thy God with all thy heart." Then He added: "The second is like unto it, Thou shalt love thy neighbor as thyself" (see Matt. 22:35–40). Both these two commandments contain the one verb *love*. Where God is in heaven and where men are on earth, love is the royal law: love is supreme.

The Christian's love for his fellowmen has more than one purpose. First, it reveals to us our own nature, given by God, which allows us to love ourselves, and it calls us to love our neighbors with the same love. Thus we have in our heart the law to love our neighbor as ourself.

Second, it teaches us to love our neighbor because God loves him. Because everyone is made in God's image, each is the object of His compassion and love no matter how evil or disobedient he may be. Therefore, I ought to love my neighbor not merely because he is my fellowman but because God loves him and I see God's image in him. "Be ye merciful, even as your Father is merciful" (Luke 6:36). From my Father in heaven I must learn how to love—even my enemies.

Third, it teaches that the Christian's love of all mankind may rise still higher. In the realm of grace, God has reconciled us to himself so that He can apportion to us His personal love. This is the law for each child of God: He must love his brother with the same love with which Christ has loved him.

Finally, the highest thought is that even as Jesus Christ, in His great love, redeemed a world dying in misery and sin, so all those who have received this love should give themselves, even as Christ did, to love all people and devote their lives to making others partakers of this great blessedness.

Child of God, we have *reason* to love and the *wherewithal* to love our neighbor. May God write the royal law of love deep in our hearts!

The Practice of Christian Love

Love in general is of a diffusive nature and espouses the interests of others. It is so with the love of natural affection and earthly friendships. Those who truly love one another do not seek their own particular interests, but seek to know and appreciate the interests of the other. They seek not only their own things, but the things of their friends. Selfishness is a principle that contracts the heart and confines it to self, while love enlarges it and extends it to others. By love, a person's heart is so extended and enlarged that the other becomes a part of himself. He will promote the other's interest and believe his own is promoted. Where the one he loves is injured, he is injured. Yet, this love may be motivated by self-love.

There are many ways in which self-love is the source of love and friendship that arises in the natural among people. In fact, most of the love in the world arises from the principle of self-love. Everyone in some way or another loves another from this root.

In our text above, divine love is spoken of as higher or beyond the natural: it is supernatural. Divine love springs from supernatural principles. Divine love is as a plant transplanted into our souls from the garden of heaven by the Holy and Blessed Spirit of God. Divine love has its life in God and not in self. Christian love is free and disinterested (impartial and neutral). Christians love God for himself and for His own sake because they are His children. By the same manner, Christians love and seek the good of others for their sake and for God's sake. Divine love is so contrary to a selfish spirit that it reaches even the unthankful and evil, and those who injure and hate us. Divine love is entirely supernatural and Godlike.

Prayer

Dear Heavenly Father, I thank you that you have implanted the principle of self-love in all of us, and that by this principle we can measure the love that we should have for all men. Without this, life would be miserable indeed. Yet, our own love is far inferior to the divine love you want to implant in our hearts, a love that reaches beyond self-interest. Grant that more and more people will open their hearts to your redeeming grace in Christ Jesus that your divine love might be more greatly felt throughout the world. For the sake of your glorious kingdom. Amen.

God . . . hath made of one blood all nations of men.

Acts 17:26

21

National Pride

A former prime minister of England said in regard to the Boer War: "It served to maintain the principle that the minorities should not be oppressed. That is to say, all these precious lives and treasures of gold were offered up in vindication of nationality, which may be regarded as a gift of God, as the divine right of each nation, according to its special nature, to preserve and develop its individuality in the service of the common life of the world. This war will develop national feeling more intensely, increase a national consciousness, and arouse hope among the peoples who have hitherto been considered the most backward in the world. People will slowly learn that national feeling depends upon character, and character depends upon religion.

"In a struggle such as this, we cannot expect the breach to be healed at once; but we can cultivate a spirit of Christian empathy with those who differ from us, and cease to regard each other with suspicion and distrust. We can trust the honesty of each other's convictions, and take more trouble to understand one another."

His comments speak most strongly of the divine right of patriotism. Yet, we must also clearly understand that the feeling, as a merely human force, is under the power of sin. Remember Paul's words: "For every creature of God is good, and nothing to be refused, if it be received with thanksgiving: for it is sanctified by the word of God and prayer" (1 Tim. 4:4, 5). Without this sanctifying process, national feeling may become the prey of ambition, and be the source of hatred, aversion, and contempt for other nations.

In Christ, God has placed all people under the law of divine love. Love is the holy calling of every Christian and more especially of every minister of the gospel. Under the guidance of the Holy Spirit, we should point out to others the way by which national pride may attain its twofold aim: first, the development and uplifting of the people themselves; and second, the right attitude toward other peoples for the building up of all mankind.

The Practice of Christian Love

Jesus Christ must be our example with respect to loving all people and nations. Christ set His love on those who were His enemies. His enemies had no love for Him and were full of enmity, bitterness, and hatred. Scripture declares: "But God commendeth his love toward us, in that, while we were yet sinners, Christ died for us. For if, when we were enemies, we were reconciled to God by the death of his Son, much more, being reconciled, we shall be saved by his life" (Rom. 5:8, 10).

Such was Christ's love for us that He was pleased in some respects to look upon us as upon himself. If we accept His love, He will unite His heart to us and be pleased to regard us as He regards himself. In His love He has sought to unite us to himself so as to make us members of His body.

Such was His love for us that He spent himself for our sakes. His love did not rest in mere feeling, in easy efforts or small sacrifices. Though we were His enemies, He loved us from His heart—denied himself, made the supreme effort, and withstood the greatest suffering for our sakes. He gave up His own ease, comfort, interest, honor and wealth. He became poor, outcast and despised. He had no place to lay His head. And all for us! Not only so, but He shed His own blood for us and offered himself a sacrifice to God's justice—that we might be forgiven, accepted and saved.

Christ knew that we would never be able to repay Him for His kindness to us. He knew that we were poor, miserable and empty-handed outcasts who could only receive from Him.

Our love should not depend on others' love in return. We should love them in the state that Christ loved us—unworthy and unlovely, enemies of God. We should endeavor to be interested in their good, as Christ is in ours. We should be willing, as Christ did for us, to part with our own time and possessions for the sake of others—and ready to do these things without hope of thanks or reciprocation. If we have this Spirit of Christ, we shall not be under the influence of a selfish spirit.

Prayer

Dear Heavenly Father, thank you for the promise that people from every tribe and nation will proclaim Jesus Christ as Lord and Savior. We know from your Word that in heaven there will be some of every nationality. Help me always to put my love of country in its proper place. While remaining loyal to my nation, help me to love all other nationalities as Christ loves them, for the sake of His coming kingdom. Amen.

I will take the stick . . . of Ephraim . . . and the stick of Judah, and make them one stick, and they shall be one in mine hand.

Ezek. 37:19

22

One Stream or Two?

If anyone were to ask me: "In which of these two do you believe?" I would answer: "In both." "And why?" "Because God has willed it so." When the small stream of the Africander people, with a population of less than one million, was turned into the mighty stream of the British Empire, with its three hundred million, God willed this should happen. He willed that in the great stream there should be two streams side by side. The two nationalities, the smaller as well as the greater, each have their own history, their own national characteristics, their own special virtues and shortcomings. In God's plan and council there was room for both.

Why has there been such terrible strife and discord over the question: one stream or two streams? Because people would not accept both viewpoints and accord to each its right. They wanted one or the other exclusively in the forefront. A person who really desires to know and do God's will—in His dealings with our people—must try to understand his twofold calling: to be faithful in preserving his own nationality and at the same time show his love and appreciation for the other nationality with whom his lot has been cast under God's providence.

When Ephraim and Judah became one in God's hand, the difference between the two was not destroyed. Each kept his own characteristics. But the oneness was that of true unity and mutual love. "Ephraim shall not envy Judah, and Judah shall not vex Ephraim." God will fulfill this promise to us—but on one condition: We must place our people in God's hand by our prayers. "They shall be one in mine hand." By means of intercession, let us place our people in God's hand. He can and will give the love and mutual forbearance that is needed.

The Practice of Christian Love

By your very profession as a Christian, you are united to Christ and to your fellow Christians. Christ and all Christians are so united together that they all make one body. Of this body, Jesus Christ is the head and Christians are the members. "We, being many, are one body in Christ, and every one members one of another," says the Apostle Paul (Rom. 12:5). And again he declares, "By one Spirit are we all baptized into one body, whether we be Jews or Gentiles, whether we be bond or free" (1 Cor. 12:13).

How unbecoming, therefore, when Christians are selfish! How shameful when they are concerned only for their own private interests! Naturally, the hand is ready to serve the head, and all the members of our bodies are ready to serve one another. Our hands do nothing for their own advantage. Our hands work day by day for the common good of our whole bodies. So it should be with the Christian body. All its members should be helpers and comforters of each other, promote their mutual welfare and happiness, and so promote the glory of Christ the head.

You are not your own. You have not made yourself, nor were you made *for* yourself. You do not uphold your own existence, nor are you dependent solely upon yourself. Another has made you, preserves you, and provides for you. You are dependent upon Him, and He has made you for himself and for the good of your fellow creatures—not only for yourself. God has placed before you higher and nobler goals and purposes than self, even the welfare of your fellowman, society, nation, the interests of His kingdom. For all of these things you ought to labor and live not only in time but for eternity.

"Ye are not your own; for ye are bought with a price . . . with the precious blood of Christ" (see 1 Cor. 6:19, 20 and 1 Pet. 1:19). Christians should not seek praise for themselves but for the glory of Jesus Christ. Christ has redeemed you, so you are His by purchase. Nothing that you have is your own: your abilities, possessions, time, talents, influence, comforts—these are for the honor of Christ and for the good of your fellowman.

Prayer

Dear Heavenly Father, though my own situation may not be as the one in South Africa—either in Andrew Murray's day or today, help me to learn from history so as not to repeat the same mistakes. Help us all to avoid the extremes of nationalism and racism on the one hand and the blurring of all distinctions on the other. So much can be learned from all nations and races as we love one another and serve one another through Jesus Christ, and not from selfish motives. Help us as Christians of various nationalities and denominations to work together naturally as your body for the sake of your kingdom. Amen.

The Lord make you to increase and abound in love one toward another, and toward all men, even as we do toward you: to the end he may stablish your hearts unblameable in holiness.

1 Thess. 3:12, 13

23
Pray for Love

What a prayer! May the Lord make us abound in love toward each other. May the Lord make all Christians increase in love toward all people, even as Paul loved those to whom he wrote. May God strengthen our hearts to be unblamable in holiness. Without love this is impossible. Our hearts must be strengthened for a life of true holiness through the love of the brethren by the power of God. Let us use this prayer often—for ourselves and for those around us. Do you pray for holiness? If so, show it by a hearty love to the brethren.

In 2 Thess. 3:5, we read: "The Lord direct your hearts into the love of God." Yes, that is what the Lord Jesus will do for us. He will give us a heart always directed to the love of God. Lord, by Thy great love, grant me a heart of love! "Always in every prayer of mine for you all making request with joy. I pray that your love may abound yet more and more in knowledge . . . that ye may be filled with the fruits of righteousness" (Phil. 1:4–11). The apostle, in his constant prayer for those in his charge, makes love the chief aim. Let us do the same.

"I would that ye knew what great conflict I have for you

. . . that [your] hearts might be comforted, being knit together in love, and unto all riches of the full assurance of understanding" (Col. 2:1, 2). Paul considered it indispensable for growth in the knowledge of God that our hearts should be knit together in love for all believers. God is love—everlasting, endless love. That love can only be experienced when Christians are knit together in love, and live for others, not only for themselves.

These four prayers of Paul give us abundant matter for meditation and prayer. Take time to let these heavenly thoughts grow in your heart. As the sun freely gives its light and heat to the grass and grain that they may grow and bring forth fruit, so God is even more willing to give His love to us in ever-increasing measure. Oh, Christian, if you feel as if you cannot pray, take these words of divine love and ponder them in your heart! You will gain a strong and joyous assurance of what God is able to do for you. He will make you to abound in love and strengthen your heart to live before Him in holiness and love of the brethren. Lord, teach us so to pray!

The Practice of Christian Love

If you will devote yourself to God and make a sacrifice of all your own interests to Him, you will not throw yourself away. Though you seem to neglect, deny and overlook yourself in imitating the divine love of God, *God will take care of you!* God will see to it that your own interests are provided for and your welfare is secure.

You will not lose by all the sacrifices you have made for God. To His glory, let it be said, He will not be your debtor. He will requite you a hundredfold even in this life, besides the eternal rewards that He will bestow upon you hereafter. He has declared: "Every one that hath forsaken houses, or brethren, or sisters, or father, or mother, or wife, or children, or lands, for my name's sake, shall receive an hundredfold, and shall inherit everlasting life" (Matt. 19:29). The spirit of this declaration applies to all sacrifices made for Christ or our fellowmen for His sake. The greatness of the reward for this life Christ expressed by a definite number; but He does not make use of numbers, however great, to set forth the reward promised hereafter. He only says they shall receive eternal life. The reward of eternal life is so great, and so exceeds all the expense of self-denial people can make for Christ's sake, that numbers are insufficient to describe it.

If you are selfish and make yourself and your own private interests your idol, then God will leave you to yourself. He will allow you to promote your own interests as well as you can. But if you do not selfishly seek your own, and *do* seek the things that are Christ's and how you may serve others, then God will make your interests and happiness His own responsibility. He is infinitely more able to provide for and promote it than you are. The resources of the universe move at His bidding and He can easily command them all to serve your welfare.

Not to seek your own in the selfish sense is the best way of seeking your own in the better sense. It is the most direct course you can take toward securing your highest happiness. If you place your happiness in God in glorifying and serving Him by doing good, you will promote your wealth, honor and pleasure here below and obtain hereafter a crown of unfading glory with pleasures at the right hand of God.

Prayer

Dear Heavenly Father, help me to live and love as your Son demonstrated when He walked upon this earth. Help me to love and serve others in such a way so as to encourage them to love and serve you through the presence of Jesus Christ in their lives. I want to put your interests and the interests of others before my own. You are the sole provider of all my needs. All glory, praise and honor belongs to your name. Amen.

I have given you an example, that ye should do as I have done to you.

John 13:15

24
Like Christ

The love of Christ, manifested in His death on the cross, is the only ground for our hope of salvation, and it is also the only rule for our daily life and conduct. Our Lord says clearly: "Ye should do as I have done." My only hope of salvation is the love of Christ, and the way to truly and fully enjoy that salvation is to walk in His love.

The Apostle Paul wrote, "Let every one of us please his neighbor for his good to edification. For even Christ pleased not himself. Wherefore receive ye one another, as Christ also received us" (Rom. 15:2, 3, 7). God will work the power within us to "receive . . . one another, as Christ also received us." He will do it for every upright soul, and for all who pray in confident faith.

Again Paul commanded, "Be ye therefore followers of God, as dear children; and walk in love, as Christ also hath loved us, and hath given himself for us" (Eph. 5:1, 2). Once again, love is everything. Realizing that we are God's dear children because Christ loved us even unto death makes it not only possible, but certain, that we should walk in love.

To amplify this thought further, read Paul's admonition: "Put on therefore, as the elect of God, holy and beloved . . .

mercy, kindness, humbleness of mind, meekness, longsuffering; forbearing one another, and forgiving one another . . . even as Christ forgave you, so also do ye. And above all these things put on [love], which is the bond of perfectness" (Col. 3:12–14). What a blessed life we have in the love and power of Christ! What a blessed walk in His fellowship when we are led by the Holy Spirit and strengthened for a life in His likeness!

O God, the Father of love, the Father of Christ, our Father, wilt Thou indeed strengthen us each day to love one another in Christ, even as He loved us!

The Practice of Christian Love

Love is naturally opposed to all wickedness or evil practice. It rather tends to all righteousness or holy practice. Love is the sum of all true and saving grace.

If you have the notion that grace is something put in your heart to be confined and dormant so that its influence does not govern your outward life, you are mistaken.

Jesus Christ, by His merits, suffering and death, has purchased grace for us that we might walk in holiness of life. He prayed, "I sanctify myself, that they also might be sanctified through the truth" (John 17:19). He has reconciled us to God by His death to save us from wickedness that we might be holy and unblamable in our lives (see Col. 1:21, 22). And for this purpose He offered himself, without spot, through the eternal Spirit, to God the Father that His blood might purge our conscience from dead works to serve the living God (see Heb. 9:14).

By His Spirit and through His truth, God calls, awakens, convicts, converts, and imparts His grace to all those who are His so that they might exercise themselves in holy living. The apostle declared: "We are his workmanship, created in

Christ Jesus unto good works, which God hath before ordained that we should walk in them" (Eph. 2:10). And he tells the Thessalonians that God had not called them unto uncleanness but unto holiness (see 1 Thess. 4:7).

A true knowledge of God and of divine things is a practical knowledge. Many unconverted people have a speculative knowledge of God and the Christian faith, but *saving* knowledge is practical and not speculative. If you have a right and saving understanding of divine things, if you see the excellency of holiness and the beauty of God, the hatefulness of sin and all its ways, certainly you will avoid evil and follow the way of holiness.

Prayer

Dear Heavenly Father, thank you for your word of truth and the example of your Son, Jesus Christ; and for the admonitions of the Apostle Paul and his loving example. Help me to love and live as they did, seeking the way of holiness. Help me to be the example you would have me be through the grace of your indwelling Holy Spirit. This I ask for the sake of your kingdom on earth. Amen.

The words that I speak unto you, they are spirit, and they are life.

John 6:63

Ye received the word of God . . . as it is in truth, the word of God, which effectually worketh also in you that believe.

1 Thess. 2:13

The word of God is quick and powerful [living and active].

Heb. 4:12

25
The Power of God's Word

The question constantly persists: *Why do God's children so little realize the great value and absolute necessity of brotherly love?* Some say, "Because of unbelief." Without faith, great faith, persevering faith, there can be no thought of the power of love within us. True faith is different from what we usually mean when we say we believe in God's Word. True faith is deeper and higher. A person with true faith bows before God in the deep realization of His greatness, of His power to work wonders in our hearts, and of His loving care for us. The word of a king or a general has great influence over his soldiers. How great beyond compare is the Word of the infinite and almighty God!

We must be deeply convinced of our inability apart from God to produce the holy love that can conquer sin and unbelief. We need a burning desire to receive this heavenly love into our hearts whatever the cost may be. At length we shall gain an insight into what God's Word is as a living power in our hearts. This supernatural power will be the love of God shed abroad in our hearts by the Holy Spirit living and working within us.

In the following devotional meditations we shall consider verses from the First Epistle of John, verses in which the love of God is promised to believers. Ask yourself if you are ready to acknowledge your deep sinfulness and lack of power. Are you ready to yield your heart unreservedly to God for this love to take possession of you? Take time in God's presence. Wait on Him in confidence that His Word will work effectively in you as a seed of new life. Then you shall love the Lord Jesus and your brethren with the same love God has for you.

The Practice of Christian Love

The principle of grace is a principle of life. Those who have grace are represented in Scripture as being alive or having the principle of life within them. Natural men have no principle of grace in their hearts and are therefore represented as dead men.

True Christian grace is not only a principle of life but an exceedingly powerful principle. Hence we read of the power of godliness (2 Tim. 3:5). True faith is a faith that works; whereas a false faith is barren and inoperative. Therefore, the Apostle Paul describes saving faith as a "faith which worketh by love" (Gal. 5:6). And the Apostle James tells us, "A man may say, Thou hast faith, and I have works: show me thy faith without thy works, and I will show thee my faith by my works" (James 2:18).

The conviction of the understanding and judgment that is implied in saving faith tends to holy practice. If you have true faith, you will be convinced of the reality and certainty of the great truths and practices of Christianity; you will be influenced by them and they will govern your actions and behavior. If you are really convinced about the truth of the gospel, about an eternal world and the everlasting salvation that Christ has purchased for all who will accept it, these beliefs will influence your practice. Your actions will be according to your convictions. Your very nature forbids that it should be otherwise.

The act of the will that there is in saving faith also tends to holy practice. If you, by the act of your will, truly accept Christ as Savior, then you also accept Him as a Savior from *sin* and not merely from the *punishment* of sin. You have not heartily received Christ as Savior if you do not sincerely will and aim in heart and life to turn from all the ways of sin. If you have received Christ by a living faith, then He is your Lord and King to rule over you and reign in you. If you have saving faith, you will not make Christ a mere atoning priest for your sins, but you will submit to His law, obey His authority, and follow His commands. You will, in short, live a life of holiness.

Prayer

Dear Heavenly Father, help me to live a holy life through the saving influence of your Word and Spirit. I have made Jesus Christ my Lord and King. I have received Him as my Savior. Reveal to me any thoughts and actions I may have which are not holy that I might forsake them. Protect me from saying and doing anything that would bring disgrace to you and to the gospel message which proclaims the transformation of any who will believe in you for Jesus' sake. Amen.

He that loveth his brother abideth in the light.

1 John 2:10

Whosoever doeth not righteousness is not of God, neither he that loveth not his brother. For this is the message that ye heard from the beginning, that we should love one another. . . . We know that we have passed from death unto life, because we love the brethren. . . . Hereby perceive we the love of God, because he laid down his life for us: and we ought to lay down our lives for the brethren. . . . And this is his commandment, That we should believe on the name of his Son Jesus Christ, and love one another.

1 John 3:10–11, 14, 16, 23

Beloved, if God so loved us, we ought also to love one another. . . . If we love one another, God dwelleth in us, and his love is perfected in us. We have known and believed the love that God hath to us. God is love; and he that dwelleth in love dwelleth in God, and God in him. . . . If a man say, I love God, and hateth his brother, he is a liar: for he that loveth not his brother whom he hath seen, how can he love God whom he hath not seen? And this commandment have we from him, That he who loveth God love his brother also.

1 John 4:11–12, 16, 20–21

26

Perfect Love According to 1 John

Each of these words is a living seed. They have within them a divine power to take root, grow, and bear fruit in our hearts. But just as a seed requires that the soil in which it grows be kept free of all weeds, so the heart must be wholly surrendered to God and His service so the seed of the Word may bear this heavenly fruit.

Read again: "And this is his commandment, That we should believe on the name of his Son Jesus Christ, and love one another" (1 John 3:23). Faith in God and love of the brethren is necessary for our salvation. Love to God and love to the brethren are inseparable: "And this commandment have we from him, That he who loveth God love his brother also" (1 John 4:21).

The Practice of Christian Love

Saving faith implies a true trust in God that tends to holy practice. Holy practice distinguishes true trust from false. Trusting God while you are negligent tempts God. Trusting

God while you are in sin is presumptuous. If you truly and rightly trust God in the way of salvation, you trust Him in the way of diligence and holiness. Living in the full persuasion of His sufficiency and faithfulness, you are ready to venture out in action relying on Him.

Love is an active principle. Love to our fellowmen always influences us in our actions and practice. The person who loves money is influenced by that love and remains in a continual pursuit of wealth. Those who love carnal desires pursue them in their practice. If you sincerely love your brethren, you will tend to practice holy deeds of love. The practice of love is the only love that will profit you. If you love God, you will be influenced by that love in your practice. If you love God, you will constantly seek after Him in the course of your life. You will seek His grace, acceptance, and glory.

Reason teaches that actions are the most proper test and evidence of love. If you profess a great deal of love and friendship to another, reason teaches that you must show evidence of a real and hearty love by your actions. You must profess your love in words and be willing to deny yourself for your friend and suffer for his interests if need be. If we see a person who by his constant behavior shows himself ready and takes pains to give his all for God, reason teaches that this is evidence that He loves God. This evidence is to be depended upon more than if he only professes that he feels a great love for God in his heart. A false hope will tend to licentiousness, to encourage people in their sinful desires and lusts, to flatter and embolden them while they are in the way of evil. A true hope of salvation will stir people up to holiness of life, awaken them to responsibility, make them careful to avoid sin and more diligent to serve a living God and their fellowman.

Prayer

Dear Heavenly Father, help me to teach the way of holiness and love by being an example in my own behav-

ior. Help me to show my true love for you and others by my pursuits and in the things that consume my attention and conversation. As others observe my life and example, help them to judge that I do love you with all my heart and others as your Son Jesus loves me. May their observations inspire them to give you the love and glory you deserve. For the sake of your coming and glorious kingdom. Amen.

Walk in love, as Christ also hath loved us, and hath given himself for us.

Eph. 5:2

27
The Love That Suffers

Do you think it strange that love, which is the source of the greatest happiness, should also be the cause of the most intense suffering? Our life on earth is such that suffering is inevitable, for love seeks to save the object of its love. It is only by means of suffering that love can gain its end and so attain the highest happiness.

What a wonderful thought! Even the almighty power of God's love could not achieve its purpose without suffering. For it was by means of His sufferings that Christ bore and overcame the sins of the whole world, and the hard heart of man was softened and drawn to God. So love in the midst of suffering manifested the greatest glory and attained its end perfectly.

Let no one, with such an example before him, imagine that love is self-sufficient. Love worthy of the name manifests itself in a life of continual self-sacrifice. Love's strength lies in renunciation. Just think what a mother suffers when a son falls into evil ways. Love gives her strength to endure, whatever the circumstances may be. Think, too, what one must undergo who has yielded himself wholeheartedly to intercede for others. It may mean tears and heartache and much wrestling in prayer. But love overcomes all obstacles.

Oh, Christian, do you really long to know the love of Christ in all its fullness? Then yield yourself wholly to Him and His blessed service. Regard yourself as a channel through which the Highest Love can attain His aim. Take the souls around you into a caring, loving heart and begin to suffer with them and intercede for them. Let it be your chief delight to live and to suffer for others in the love and fellowship of the Lord Jesus. Then at length you will realize what this life of love is as a servant of God—and, even as Christ did, will live wholly for the welfare and happiness of others.

Oh, believer, dwell on this wonderful truth, that there can be no real fellowship in the love of Christ except in unreserved surrender to seek always the glory of God in the salvation of your fellowman. "He that dwelleth in love dwelleth in God, and God in him" (1 John 4:16).

The Practice of Christian Love

Do you find that you particularly delight in Christian behavior as distinct from worldly morality?

By Christian behavior, I mean a meek, humble, prayerful, self-denying, self-renouncing lifestyle. Some of the heathen philosophers wrote of justice, generosity and fortitude, but they were far from a Christian poverty of spirit and lowliness of mind. They sought their own glory and gloried exceedingly in their outward virtues. But they seemed to know nothing of a walk such as the gospel commands—that of self-denial and prayerful reliance on God. They were strangers to meekness, and did not allow or even dream that to forgive an enemy was a virtue. Are you essentially distinguished and different in your spirit from the mere moralist or heathen philosopher? A true and faithful Christian makes holiness his great concern, not a mere incidental thing.

Suffering in the cause of Jesus Christ is a fruit of Christian love. It goes beyond a mere morality. A truly Christian spirit will make us willing to undergo all the sufferings to which we may be exposed for the cause of Christ. Hypocrites may make a great show of words and deeds, but they are not likely to be willing to suffer for Christ's sake.

Are you willing to suffer the loss of your good name for Christ's sake?—or to suffer reproach and contempt for the love of the brethren? Do you prefer the honor of Christ to your own? Do you have the disposition to suffer hatred and the criticism of others as Christ foretold, and are you willing to suffer the loss of your possessions if need be? Like the Apostle Paul, are you willing to endure hardship, fatigue, afflictions, distresses, stripes, imprisonments, tumults, labors, watchings, and fastings for the Christian faith? The willingness to suffer all these things for the sake of God and others is the fruit of Christian love and has nothing to do with pagan wisdom.

Prayer

Dear Heavenly Father, forgive me when I may think that faith is a tool to escape the suffering that love and responsibility as a Christian may sometimes demand. Help me to be willing to suffer for others, and thus show my true love for you and them, even as Jesus was willing to suffer and die for the sake of mankind. Amen.

Now the works of the flesh are manifest, which are these, Adultery, fornication, uncleanness, lasciviousness, idolatry, witchcraft, hatred, variance, emulations, wrath, strife, seditions, heresies, envyings, murders, drunkenness, revellings, and such like: of the which I tell you before, as I have also told you in time past, that they which do such things shall not inherit the kingdom of God.

Gal. 5:19–21

28

The Works of the Flesh

In these three verses, Paul mentions seventeen "works of the flesh." Nine of these are sins against love. And he says elsewhere, "Let all bitterness, and wrath, and anger, and clamor, and evil speaking, be put away from you, with all malice" (Eph. 4:31). Here he answers the question why there is so little love among Christians and why it is so hard to promote such love.

Even the earnest Christian is still in the flesh. Paul says: "For I know that in me (that is, in my flesh,) dwelleth no good thing" (Rom. 7:18). It is quite impossible for a Christian by his own efforts to lead a life of love. Scripture says, "Walk in the Spirit, and ye shall not fulfil the lust of the flesh" (Gal. 5:16). The Spirit will enable us to keep the flesh always in subjection. The "fruit of the Spirit" will be Christ's love poured into our hearts as a fountain of love. Paul adds: "The law of the Spirit of Life in Christ Jesus hath made me free from the law of sin" (Rom. 8:2). The grace of God will enable the Christian to walk, not after the flesh, but after the Spirit.

Learn these three great lessons: (1) The Christian cannot in his own strength love God and his fellowman. (2) The great reason for so much bitterness and lack of love is that the Christian walks after the flesh. (3) The only sure way to abide in this life of love, to love God and Christ with the whole heart, to love the brethren fervently, and to have a tender, compassionate love for all who do not yet know Christ—is to absolutely surrender to the Holy Spirit and to be led and guided by Him each day of our lives. Through the Holy Spirit this love is shed abroad in our hearts.

The Holy Spirit will take entire possession of you and will work continually within you a life of love to Christ and to all people. Pray for this until it becomes a reality.

The Practice of Christian Love

All the graces of Christianity are from the same Spirit. As the Apostle Paul says, "There are diversities of gifts, but the same Spirit . . . diversities of operation, but it is the same God which worketh all in all" (1 Cor. 12:4, 6). All the graces of Christianity are from the same Spirit of Christ sent forth into the heart and dwelling there as the divine nature. Grace in the heart is the Holy Spirit in action, communicating His own holy nature.

There are not *many* conversions of the soul, such as one to faith, one to love of God, one conversion to humility, another to repentance, and still another to the love of others. No. All these graces are produced by one and the same work of the Spirit, and are the result of one and the same conversion or change of heart. All the graces are united and linked together—contained in the same new nature that is given to us in regeneration.

The sight or sense of God's excellency begets faith, love, repentance and all the other graces. Those who truly know God's nature will love Him, trust Him, submit to Him, serve and obey Him.

A true Christian, the moment he is converted, possesses

not one or two holy principles but the whole gracious disposition of Christ. His first efforts at its manifestation may be feeble, like the faculties of an infant, but the disposition is there and will be seen flowing out progressively toward both God and others. All true converts are renewed in Christ's image.

Faith replaces unbelief, love displaces enmity, humility swallows up pride, and meekness mortifies revenge. As one of the graces takes its place in the heart, the opposite gives way, just as darkness in a room vanishes when a light is brought in. Old things pass away. Conversion is a great work and produces a great change!

Prayer

Dear Heavenly Father, by your Holy Spirit, bear in me each day the fruits of love in my life to overcome any pride and unbelief that may remain. Remind me that I can do nothing in my own strength, but must rely wholly upon the Spirit of Christ dwelling in me. Whenever I am tempted to mind the flesh and follow my own desires, bring me back to the life of holiness you have called us all to, that your kingdom may come upon earth and your will be done as it is in heaven. Amen.

But let it be the hidden man of the heart, in that which is not corruptible, even the ornament of a meek and quiet spirit, which is in the sight of God of great price. . . . Finally, be ye all of one mind, having compassion one of another; love as brethren, be pitiful, be courteous.

1 Pet. 3:4, 8

29

The Love of God in Women

God created man to show the power of love that strives for the welfare of others, to the giving up of one's life for them. He created woman to show what tenderness and quiet endurance are: her sacrifice for the sake of her family. A little child, during the first years of his life, is dependent upon his mother, and the mother is thereby trained in the school of self-sacrificing love—for her greatest adorning is "the ornament of a meek and quiet spirit, which is in the sight of God of great price" (1 Pet. 3:4).

The tendency today in public life is to place women on equal footing with men. This is only right in many cases. But one must not forget that the best ornament of a woman is a meek and quiet spirit, which is of great price in the sight of God and man, and which enables her to be a blessing in her home. The self-denying, prayerful, all-conquering love of the wife and the mother secures the happiness of a home and of a people.

Dear sisters, preserve as a great treasure the precious jewel that God has entrusted to you—to reflect the love of God in all its tenderness and sympathy. "As one whom his mother comforteth, so will I comfort you" (Isa. 66:13). Let each woman, as she reads this book, take time to meditate on God's wonderful love and pray for it earnestly in a receptive spirit. This will give you a heavenly influence upon your husband and children; and in your dealings with your neighbors, you will be a living witness to what the love of God can do.

Think of Mary, the woman who loved much, and the other women to whom the Lord revealed himself on the resurrection morning. The love of these women gave them the privilege of being the first to meet the Lord and to take the news of His resurrection to His disciples.

God bless mothers, wives and daughters! May they prove by their lives how beautiful and powerful the love of a woman can be!

The Practice of Christian Love

Every expression of holy love that is or ever was proceeds from God. God the Father, God the Son, and God the Holy Spirit dwell in heaven united as one in infinitely mutual, incomprehensible, and eternal love. God the Father is the father of mercies, who loved the world so much He gave His only begotten Son.

The Lamb of God, the Prince of Peace and Love, so loved the world that He shed His blood and died on the cross. As the great Mediator, He expresses divine love toward us and imparts love to the hearts of all God's people, enabling them to fulfill their roles on earth of love and service to all those with whom they have to do.

The Holy Spirit, the Spirit of divine love, from whom the very essence of God flows, sheds this love abroad into the hearts of all the saints. No one's true expression of love is his own, but comes from God.

Prayer

Dear Jesus, I cannot fathom the depths of human love: the love of husband and wife, the love of parent and child, the love of brother and sister. I cannot comprehend the depth of love a Christian has for another Christian. How can I even begin to understand your love for your Father and the Holy Spirit, your love for the angels and saints in heaven, your love for me and your brethren on earth? Help me to think about the depth of your love and be motivated by your Spirit to love more and more each day. Amen.

Let a man so account of us, as of the ministers of Christ, and stewards of the mysteries of God. Moreover it is required in stewards, that a man be found faithful.

1 Cor. 4:1, 2

30

Stewards of the Love of God

A steward is a man to whom the king or master entrusts his treasures and goods so he can apportion them to those who have a right to them. God in heaven needs people on earth to reveal the treasures of His love, and to give them to those who have need. A minister of the gospel is a steward of the mysteries of God. He is a steward of the deep mystery of His everlasting love and all the blessings that flow from it.

Stewards must be found faithful: they must devote themselves wholly to their life task. They must be faithful at their work, and always be at their post in the palace or house where the treasures are stored. So the minister of the gospel himself must be faithful, living each day in the love and fellowship of God. He must be faithful to God and to his fellowman, caring for the needs of the souls entrusted to him, ready to recommend God's love and to share it with others. This divine love is a mystery and can only dwell in a heart set apart for God and satisfied with His love, which flows from Him as a stream of living water.

Oh, child of God, seek to have a deeper insight into what the office of a servant of God means, as a steward of the wonderful love of God to sinners. Pray much and often for your ministers that God may hide them in the secret of His tabernacle, so that they may be faithful stewards of the mystery of God and chiefly of the mystery of divine love.

And you, my beloved brethren, to whom the love of God in heaven and of Christ on the cross is entrusted, remember that your congregation, your church, your people are dependent on your faithfulness in living a holy life in fellowship with God. Then you will be able with joy, and in the power of the Holy Spirit, to pass on the love of God to souls that so greatly need it.

The Practice of Christian Love

From the love that is within them, true Christians will endeavor to live in heart and life, in principle and in practice, a life of holiness. Divine love makes them long for holiness and thirst after spiritual growth. Christians long for greater oneness with God and one another, for true liberty and better fruit. Love is a holy fire within him—and, like any flame, it consumes him.

Fix your eye upon Jesus. Look to Him as your example. Consider how He patiently continued in well-doing even when He was not honored and acknowledged as the Son of God. Look to Him as your Mediator. Trust in the atonement He has made for you. He is your Intercessor, who forever pleads for you before the throne of God that the Spirit may enable you to press on and overcome every difficulty of the way.

Prayer

Dear Heavenly Father, I want to be a good steward of the treasures of the gospel that you have entrusted to me. I want to share those truths with others which will enable them to share in the wonderful fruits of the Holy Spirit. Help me to love you and others with a perfect holy love that I might not be found wanting as your servant. Help me keep my eyes upon Jesus, the author and finisher of my faith. Amen.

In Jesus Christ neither circumcision availeth anything, nor uncircumcision; but faith which worketh by love.

Gal. 5:6

31

Faith Working Through Love

Faith is the root; love is the fruit. Faith becomes strong in the love of God and of Christ. Faith in God and love to the brethren must always go hand in hand. Faith in God's wonderful love, shed abroad in our hearts, enables us to live always in love toward our fellowman. This true faith gives us power for a life of fervent, all-embracing love.

Yet how little the Church realizes all this! How seldom does the preacher lay stress on a Christlike love to the brethren as the fruit and joy of the life of faith!

All of our life—in the home, between father and mother, parents and children, brothers and sisters, friends and servants—should be a life in the love of Christ. Do not say: *"It is impossible."* All things are possible to God, who through His Holy Spirit will shed His love into our hearts to be lived out in our daily lives. Let our faith cling to God's Word and to the unseen and wonderful things He will do for us each day. Let these thoughts about love impel us to accept with new and greater faith the love of God, and then dedicate our lives to letting it radiate from us to all people, yes, even to our enemies, and to the unbelievers in the uttermost parts of the earth.

Oh, Christian, the whole of salvation lies in these two words: faith and love. Let our faith each day take deeper root in God's eternal love. And then each day the fruit of the Spirit will be love in all our dealings with those around us. May God imprint these words deeply in our hearts, and make them a joy and strength to us: *In Jesus Christ nothing avails but "love working through faith."*

The Practice of Christian Love

See that you live a life of love—of love to God and love to others. All of us hope to have part in the world of love hereafter; therefore, here on earth we should cherish the Spirit of Love and live a life of holy love. This is the way to be like the inhabitants of heaven, who are now confirmed in love forever. Only in this way can you be like them in excellence and loveliness, in happiness, rest and joy.

By living in love in this world, you may be like the inhabitants of heaven in sweet and holy peace; and thus have on earth a foretaste of heavenly pleasures and delights. Here, you may have a sense of the glory of heavenly things, as of God and Christ and holiness. Here, your heart may be disposed and opened by holy love to God and by the Spirit of Peace and Love to others, to sense the excellence and sweetness of all that is found in heaven. Thus shall the windows of heaven be opened so that its glorious light may shine in upon your soul. Thus you may have the evidence of your fitness for that blessed world, knowing that you are actually on the way to its possession.

Turn the stream of your thoughts and affections toward heaven, the world of love, and toward the God of love who dwells there, and toward the saints and angels who are at

Christ's right hand. Let your thoughts also be much on the objects and enjoyments of the world of love. Commune much with God and Christ in prayer. Think often of all that is in heaven, of your friends who are there, and of the praises and worship that are there, and of all that will make up the blessedness of that world of love. "Let your conversation be in heaven."

Happy, thrice happy, are those who are found faithful to the end and then welcomed to the joy of their Lord! There "they shall hunger no more, neither thirst any more; neither shall the sun light on them, nor any heat. For the Lamb which is in the midst of the throne shall feed them, and shall lead them unto living fountains of waters: and God shall wipe away all tears from their eyes" (Rev. 7:16, 17).

Prayer

Dear Heavenly Father, keep my heart and mind stayed upon you and heavenly things; fill me with your Spirit and your love that I might be enabled to serve others here upon this earth in the name of your Son. Dear Father, strengthen my faith so I can do works of love in the power of your Holy Spirit that you might be glorified in heaven and on earth in the salvation of many through Jesus Christ. May my hope always be in you. Amen.